SUSAN OWEN A

GW00367473

Discovering
Country Walks in
South London

SHIRE PUBLICATIONS LTD

Contents

Copyright © 1982 and 1991 by Susan Owen and Angela Haine. First published 1982. Second edition 1991. Number 271 in the Discovering series. ISBN 0 7478 0114 2.

Printed in Great Britain by C. I. Thomas & Sons (Haverfordwest) Ltd, Press Buildings, Merlins Bridge, Haverfordwest, Dyfed SA61 1XF.

Introduction

The walks in this book are located in a narrow belt around the south side of London, all but two being south of the river Thames. The walks are widely spaced from Windsor in the west to Chislehurst in the east. In between the concrete and glass of the buildings, on the routes nearest to the capital there are country-like walks to be found, and, for those who are interested in combining walking with a visit to a place of historical importance, the routes have been planned to go near such places as Hampton Court Palace, Ham House, Kew Palace and Osterley House. Other places of interest which can be seen en route are the Magna Carta and Kennedy memorials at Runnymede, as well as the Air Forces Memorial. In this revised edition a short alternative walk is offered to Scadbury Nature Reserve near Chislehurst.

The walks are of varying lengths from 4 to $8^{1}/_{2}$ miles, to suit the time people have at their disposal; they are all circular, with one exception, where the return to the starting point is made by train. All the walks are covered by Ordnance Survey 1:50,000 maps 176, 177, 186 or 187 and sketch maps are provided. We have given bus routes where possible and the useful publication *London Buses*, issued by London Transport, covers all the areas visited and can be obtained at bus terminals and underground stations.

Although there may be less mud and fewer wet areas than in the deepest country, we still advise the wearing of strong waterproof footwear, and even more care should be taken to observe the Countryside Code, because of the pressures on the countryside near to an area of high population, so that it is not made unsightly for those who follow in our footsteps.

We acknowledge the London Boroughs of Croydon and Richmond for their kind permission to use short extracts from some of their publications on nature trails and local history notes.

Finally, we thank Peggy Chester for helping to prepare these walks.

The cover photograph of the view of Petersham Meadows from Richmond Hill is by Cadbury Lamb. The maps were drawn by Richard G. Holmes.

British Library Cataloguing in Publication Data: Owen, Susan Discovering country walks in South London. — second edition. —1. South London. Recreations: walking. I. Title II. Haine, Angela. 796.5109416. ISBN 0-7478-0114-2

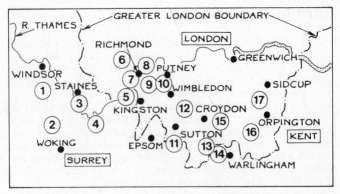

The locations of the starting points of the walks described in this book.

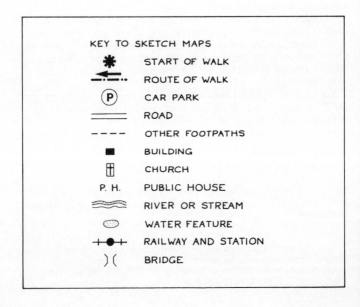

KEY TO SKETCH MAPS

✱	START OF WALK
⬅·—··	ROUTE OF WALK
Ⓟ	CAR PARK
═══	ROAD
----	OTHER FOOTPATHS
■	BUILDING
⛪	CHURCH
P. H.	PUBLIC HOUSE
〰〰	RIVER OR STREAM
⬭	WATER FEATURE
+●+	RAILWAY AND STATION
) (	BRIDGE

1. Windsor Great Park, Runnymede and Cooper's Hill

Distance: 7¹/₂ miles, or 4¹/₂ miles if omitting Runnymede and Cooper's Hill.
Grid reference: 977706.
Ordnance Survey maps: 1:50,000 sheet 176; 1:25,000 sheet SU 87/97.

This walk starts by the Obelisk in Windsor Great Park and climbs to the famous statue of George III on horseback, known as the Copper Horse, with its fine views down the Long Walk to Windsor Castle and beyond. The short walk continues through woods and parkland back to the car park whilst the longer walk leaves the park to visit the memorials to John F. Kennedy and Magna Carta and the banks of the Thames at Runnymede. A steep climb leads to the Air Forces memorial on Cooper's Hill and we return by field paths and lanes to the Savill Gardens (closed from 25th to 28th December).

Bus: (Longer walk only) 441 (High Wycombe to Staines); Green Line 718. Bus stop on Priests Hill (A328) near Englefield Green, near junction of Cooper's Hill and Ridgemead Road. Join the longer walk at (A).
Car park: Large car park for the Savill Gardens (charge), or there is room for some cars off the road about 200 years past the car park, on the right. To reach the car park, continue on the A30 past the roundabout at Egham (if coming from Staines) and turn right by a large notice about the Savill Gardens. Turn right sharply just before an inn and the car park is on the left about half a mile further on. There is also a car park on Cooper's Hill.
Refreshments: Inn near Savill Gardens or cafe at Runnymede.

From the centre of the large car park for the Savill Gardens, follow the signpost pointing towards the Obelisk and go through a small gate in the rear fence on the left. Walk a few yards to the crossing path, with a view of the Obelisk pond away to the left. Turn right towards the Obelisk, which was erected to the memory of the Duke of Cumberland, and continue down the sandy path with the pond on the left, crossing a bridge and following the wide grassy path with the Savill Gardens on the right. At the cottage ahead cross the drive and go to the left of the cottage, bending round to the right on a horse ride. Fork left on a path with a fence on to fields to the left and, after some distance, bear left towards a tennis court which can be seen ahead. Cross a drive to Cumberland Lodge and continue on the path with the tennis court immediately on the right. Just past the court, where the road bends round to the left, continue ahead on a grassy path towards the road. Go up to the junction of roads, with some seats on the left, and pass Chaplain's Lodge on the left. After a short distance, take the right-hand fork. There is a good view of the Copper Horse away to the right and the Queen Mother's residence, Royal Lodge, is hidden by the trees on the right.

At some crossroads turn right and keep on this road to a T junction, with a view of Windsor Castle and Eton College Chapel ahead. Turn right through gates and immediately take the path to the right of a horse ride leading uphill through woodland. When the fence to the plantation on the right bends round to the right, continue on the grass near the escarpment towards the Copper Horse on the top of Snow Hill, passing through a copse. The view is superb from here and you can sometimes see the yachts sailing on the large reservoirs on the right. Keep on past the rear of the statue on a wide grassy track leading into a wood and, after passing a stone bridge away down on the left, cross a grassy stretch slightly uphill to the road with a track opposite. Follow the track through the wood for some way to a junction of four tracks. Take the one opposite with a fir plantation on the right. The two walks divide some way down this track.

For the longer walk (7½ miles)

Follow the track to the end and leave Windsor Great Park past a cottage to a road. Turn right and after some way turn left down Ridgemead Road, passing a reservoir on the right. Near the end of this pleasant road take the stony path ahead down to the main road. The bus stop is on the right on the main road. (The Cooper's Hill car park is along the road opposite.)

(A) Turn left down the main road, with a view of the Queen Mary Reservoir ahead. After a short distance turn right and cross the road to go down Oak Lane. After passing some of the Brunel University outbuildings, the path leads into some woods, and soon, rather unexpectedly, we come to the stone erected in memory of John F. Kennedy 'on the acre of English ground given to the USA by the people of Britain'. Go down the steps through the wood towards the river and after passing through a gate turn right to the Magna Carta Memorial. This small temple over a plinth commemorates the Magna Carta as the symbol of freedom under law and was erected by the American Bar Association in 1957. Cross the field to the road and on to the banks of the Thames, a most popular spot for holidaymakers and picnickers in the summer. There is a cafe on the left by the entrance to Runnymede. Turn right along by the river, taking care to keep to the right when the bank is split by a small inlet. Where the inlet joins the river, cross the

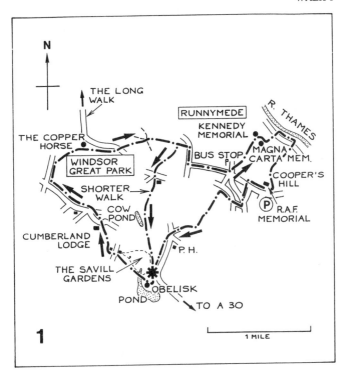

N

THE LONG WALK

RUNNYMEDE

R. THAMES

KENNEDY MEMORIAL

THE COPPER HORSE

BUS STOP

MAGNA CARTA MEM.

WINDSOR GREAT PARK

COOPER'S HILL

SHORTER WALK

COW POND

P R.A.F. MEMORIAL

CUMBERLAND LODGE

P. H.

THE SAVILL GARDENS

OBELISK

POND

TO A 30

1

1 MILE

road to a footpath sign and stile.

Follow the rather indistinct path through the water meadow towards Cooper's Hill, with the Air Forces Memorial on the brow. This meadow may be rather waterlogged in the winter. Go through the kissing gate and continue ahead to a stile. Take the path through the wood, straight up Cooper's Hill. Go through a barrier out to a road and turn right to reach the memorial. This memorial (1953) and its gardens are beautifully maintained by the War Graves Commission and on one of the walls is a prophetic couplet by Alexander Pope:

'On Cooper's Hill eternal wreaths shall grow

While lasts the Mountain, or while the Thames shall flow.'

Views of seven counties can be seen on a clear day from the top of the tower, also the aircraft taking off and landing at nearby Heathrow Airport.

On leaving the memorial, turn right to pass the car park on the left, go past a minor road on the left, and just past Brunel University car park turn left to the main road, with a common on the right. At the main road cross to Bishopsgate Road and turn right. At a bend ignore a left-hand turning and continue round another bend to turn left down Ham Lane, opposite Castle Hill Road. Continue forward on a narrow lane and, after some way, when this track bends round to the right, continue over a stile into a field and keep close to the right-hand fence. At the end of the field bear right over a stile and keep right to another stile and some steps leading down to a passage, which comes out by some cottages. At the end of the lane turn left past an inn on the left and continue for about a quarter of a mile to the car park, shop and garden centre at the Savill Gardens on the right.

For the shorter walk (4¹/₂ miles)

Continue along this track for about half a mile until you reach the crest of a rise with a cottage in the distance ahead. Ignore the path on the right at the top and go down to the next path on the right, a few yards further on. This path climbs quite steeply and after a time bends to the left, with a white house ahead. Keep to the path by the fence. On coming to open parkland, continue forward and go slightly left towards a gate in the deer fence ahead. Go through the gate and up to the white gates near the lodge. (There is an inn on the right just past the gates.) Turn right past the lodge gardens to a small wooden gate leading to a broad rhododendron walk. Keep right when the path forks, soon passing Cow Pond, a pleasant spot for a picnic. Go over the crossing track leading to the pond and, on reaching the tarmac road at the end of the Savill Gardens, continue forward to the car park.

2. Stanners Hill, Chobham and Burrowhill

Distance: 6¹/₂ miles.
Grid reference: 994635.
Ordnance Survey maps: 1:50,000 sheet 176 or 186; 1:25,000 sheet SU 86/96.

A varied walk across the common near the fishponds at Stanners Hill and then via field paths and water meadows to the attractive village of Chobham with its fine houses and cottages. The walk continues to the hamlet of Burrowhill and then on to the wild and beautiful heathland near Albury Bottom.

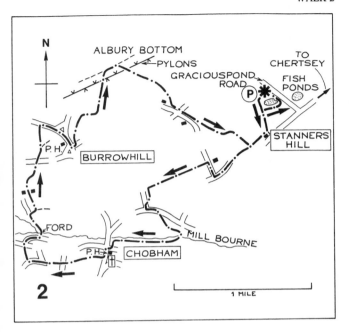

Bus: Weyfarer service 285, Guildford, Woking, Chobham and Camberley. No service on Sundays. Stop in Chobham, pick up the walk at (A).

Car park: In Gracious Pond Road. Half a mile south of Chertsey, turn off A320 on to B386 and fork left in half a mile. Gracious Pond Road is the second turning on the right, about two miles further on, and the car park is about 300 yards down on the left.

Refreshments: In Chobham and Burrowhill.

From the rear of the car park in Gracious Pond Road, take the centre path through the half gate, between notice boards. Keep on this main path leading off slightly to the left. After a short distance, bear off to the left down to the beautiful pool, popular with fishermen. In June the surface of the water is dotted with waxen waterlilies in white and deep red. Long ago the monks of Chertsey made a great pond on this common and called it Gracher's Pond, but the spelling has now changed to Gracious Pond and the site of the lake is occupied by a farm which bears its name. This fishpond, and one or two others, may also have

9

been made by the monks.

At the shores of the pond turn right through a wooden barrier and go round the head of the pond to another set of barriers. Turn right through these and continue on the path to a track by the fence ahead. Turn left along this track for some way, ignoring side turnings, until, at a junction of paths at the end of a field on the right, you turn right at a public footpath sign to follow the path between fences, with dog kennels on the left. Cross the stile and keep on in the same direction over an open field, making for a footpath sign ahead. **(B)** (If you are following the walk from Chobham, turn right at the end of the wood, cross the stile and continue the walk here.)

Keep straight on over a stile, and cross two more stiles at the top edge of two small fields to join the beginning of a farm track. Keep on this track past Chobham Park Farm and Stables. At the footpath sign turn right, passing entrance gates and turn left over a stile to cross the field to a double barred gap in the wire fence. Cross the next field in the same direction to the edge of a wood, over another barrier and follow the path on the left of a hedge down to houses. Turn left to a stile in the corner of the field. Cross this and two further stiles out to a road. Turn left down to the main road and turn left again, go round a bend and at the end of a garden on the right, take the signed path over a barrier. Follow the line of trees along the left hand edge of the field and then swing round to the right to cross a wooden bridge with barriers. Turn right to follow the path alongside the stream. After some way the stream passes the gardens of houses and bungalows and there is a good view of the tower of Chobham church ahead. The path swings round to the left, leaving the stream, and soon reaches the car park at Chobham. Turn right down the passage running beside the car park and continue towards the main road in Chobham village.

Turn left past the delightful Laurel and Cannon Cottages and the small green containing the war memorial and a cannon. There are many fine houses and cottages here and the stream we were following is now on the opposite side of the road.

(A) (Bus users start the walk here.) Keep left past the bus stop and the road leading down to Woking and go past the White Hart inn and St Lawrence's church. The church porch is believed to have come from the great abbey at Chertsey when it was dissolved by Henry VIII in 1538. Cross the pedestrian crossing to some quaint antique shops and go down a small lane past a cottage called Church View. Continue past a school and a cemetery and follow a path through a nursery garden. Cross over a track and keep on in the same direction through two fields to reach a road at a corner. The delightful cottage on the left, called Pennypot, is thought to derive its name from a former prominent resident, John de Pentecost.

Continue forward on the road for a short distance to a bridleway on the right, by the side of a broken stile. Follow the path out to a road. Cross this to take a small road opposite which swings round to the right past glasshouses. Turn left by a footpath sign on a wall, over a white footbridge by a disused ford. Follow the path by the stream up to a gate beside a stile with a footpath sign. Do not cross the stile but turn right on a wide path between fences and after a few yards turn left over a stile. Follow the path ahead to go through a gate. Turn right to a stile which leads to an enclosed path by a farm. Turn left away from the farm and in a few yards go through a gate on the right into a dark wood. Keep on the main path and go through two gates. Turn left along by the fence, passing a small brick building on the right, cross the field to the road. Cross the road to the footpath sign opposite by a stile and follow the path to another sign by a ditch. Turn right along the side of the ditch, cross a wooden plank and turn left along a path with wire netting on the right. This path leads down to a road, where you turn right and then right again at the main road leading past the Cloche Hat restaurant.

A little further on, opposite the Four Horseshoes pub, turn left down Gorse Lane by the side of the common and fork left down Heather Way. At a triangle with a telegraph pole in the centre, take the right-hand fork (the path on the left bends round to the road). Do not go down past the electricity substation on the right, but continue forward past a footpath sign. After some way turn right at a T junction and then shortly take the left fork, which emerges at a broad path. Turn left and immediately fork right on a path between a fir and a gorse bush.

This churned-up path, which has a stream running down the middle in wet weather, leads across the wild and beautiful heathland called Albury Bottom. After about a quarter of a mile, fork slightly left up a gentle slope to pass under the pylons. This path leads to a broad path at a T junction. In the distance is the ancient barrow now popular with model aircraft enthusiasts. Turn right to cross under the electricity wires again and at a fork turn right away from the pylons. Follow the path down to trees and a ditch on the left. Cross a track to a T junction and turn left with fields and farm buildings to the right. Just past a planked bridge over a stream, fork right, still with fields to the right, and shortly fork right again, keeping to the edge of the field. At a crossing track turn right. Turn left on reaching the lane, just past a very wet area. There are some riding stables on the right. Take the left fork and at a minor road ahead cross this to the drive leading up to Rambridge Farm.

When the drive swings round to the farmhouse, go to the left and follow the footpath sign over two stiles, crossing a large field towards woods ahead. Climb over the stile by a gate, cross a bridge, and follow the well marked path round to the left, skirting the edge of the wood ahead. Do not go into the wood by the stile, but keep along the edge of the wood to the footpath signs. (Those coming by bus from Chobham should turn right at the end of the wood and follow the walk from (B) at the end of the second paragraph.)

At the footpath sign turn left across the field to rejoin the outward path past the dog kennels. Turn left at the end of the path. Continue in the same direction and turn right down towards the barriers by the lake and walk along the shore with the lake on the left. Go round the end of the lake and cross between two small ponds to continue forward to the car park ahead.

3. Laleham, Staines, Thorpe and Chertsey

Distance: 8 miles.
Grid reference: 052679.
Ordnance Survey maps: 1:50,000 sheet 176; 1:25,000 sheets TQ 06/16 and TQ 07/17.

This walks follows the towpath by the Thames from Laleham into Staines and then crosses to the village of Thorpe, passing various lakes formed from disused gravel and sand workings. The path to Chertsey cuts across the centre of Thorpe Water Park with good views of some of the models and exhibits there and also the various water activities. After going through the outskirts of Chertsey, we return to Laleham along the river bank.

Buses: 459, 461. Stop near Chertsey Bridge. Walk up the road by the Thames towards Laleham. Also buses in Staines (pick up the walk at Staines river bridge).
Station: Staines (SR from Waterloo). Walk through the town to pick up the walk at Staines river bridge.
Car park: By the river at Laleham. Turn right (if coming from Shepperton) off B375 immediately before Chertsey Bridge — parking is on the right about a mile down this road.
Refreshments: In Staines, Thorpe or Chertsey.

From one of the car parks at Laleham (which become rather crowded at summer weekends), cross the road and turn right on a grassy area by the river. When this ends go forward on a 'no through road'. When the road bends sharply to the right, continue forward on the towpath to Staines for about 2$\frac{1}{4}$ miles, passing Penton Hook Lock. In the nine-

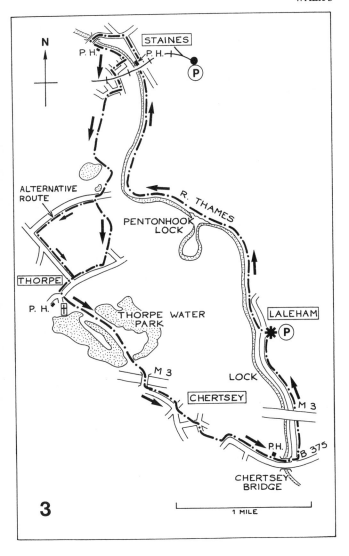

3

1 MILE

13

teenth century the fields behind Penton Hook Lock were the scene of prizefighting and the carriages of the gentry and others would wait on the far side of the river. If unruly scenes occurred and the police were called, quick escapes to avoid arrest, by fleeing to the next county on the opposite riverbank, would be made by means of one of the several ferries that operated by the lock. Sadly, they are all closed nowadays.

Leave the towpath at the railway bridge, go past the Thames Lodge Hotel (Packhorse inn) and down the side back to the towpath as far as the restaurant near Staines bridge. Go up on to the bridge and cross to the far side. (Those coming from the station and buses in Staines, join the walk here.) Go down some steps on the left, cross a footbridge and continue along the towpath a short way, passing the Swan inn. Two hundred yards or so before the railway bridge ahead, turn right up a narrow path between houses, at the end of a red brick wall with iron railings. Turn left at the minor road and then right. At the main road, turn left under the railway bridge and then immediately right down a residential road. Keep to the left down this road and, at some grassy triangles, go over a stile on the left between hedges.

Follow the path for about a mile and cross two stiles to reach a wooden bridge on the left by a lake. Cross the bridge and continue on this gravelly path past fields of horses to a large iron gate. Go across the field on a small path running beside the telegraph wires. Go under the wires in the middle of the field, keeping on in the same direction. At the far corner of the field, cross a small concrete footbridge to take the fenced path ahead, passing a large pond on the right. Cross the stile and turn right along the lane for a short distance. Just past a bungalow on the left there is a choice of paths. One can either continue forward along the lane to a road, turn left, keep ahead at a bend, go up to a T junction and turn right to Thorpe, OR cross the disused gravel pits which are now being infilled. This route is not advised in wet weather. Turn left at the bungalow and soon skirt an enormous pit on the right. About a hundred or more yards past the pit, turn right up to a rough track which leads to a fine house. Go across a field to the left of the house to a barrier with a public footpath sign by the road. Turn right along the road for about half a mile to Thorpe. This pretty country road has fine views towards St Ann's Hill on the other side of the M3 and passes between fields.

In Thorpe there is a picturesque group of old houses and cottages clustered round the church and ranging in date from the sixteenth and eighteenth centuries until the present day. On the other side of the road is a well preserved country-style house called Renalds Herne. There is an inn further down the road. At the corner, with the old church down to the left, turn sharply left over the steps and a stone barrier to an enclosed path with a footpath sign to Chertsey. This ancient path was once the connection between Thorpe and the old abbey at Chertsey and was raised above the surrounding marshy land in places. This marshy land now forms the Thorpe Water Park and the path runs through the centre of the park, giving the opportunity of seeing some of the exhibits and displays in the distance. The area on the right has been beautifully landscaped and planted with trees and shrubs, and boats are available for hire to visitors to the park. The path passes the lake used for water activities, such as regattas and water-ski competitions. After crossing a graceful bridge linking two lakes the path leads between fences towards the busy M3 and the bridge.

Go under the bridge beside the motorway and turn left at the fence to go up the path to the bridge. Turn left and cross the M3 by the bridge. On the other side, go down the public footpath which leads to a cul-de-sac. Walk along this road to a main road, with a green used for sports opposite. Cross the green, or go round the edge if matches are being played, to a minor road and turn left. At a grassy triangle surrounded with stone posts turn right up Abbey Green and at the row of houses ahead turn left to take a footpath running beside the white wall of Manor Farm Cottages, and swing right with a wooden fence on the left. One of these beautiful cottages has a plaque denoting that it is a building of historic interest. Follow this bridlepath to the main road and turn left to walk through the outskirts of Chertsey for about half a mile. Go over Chertsey bridge and turn left to follow the river past Chertsey Lock and under the motorway back to the car park on the right.

4.   Walton, Weybridge and the Wey Navigation Canal

Distance: 8^1/$_2$ miles or 7^1/$_2$ miles.
Grid reference: 093663.
Ordnance Survey maps: 1:50,000 sheet 176; 1:25,000 sheet TQ 06/16.

This walk follows the Thames from Walton to Weybridge and then diverges through Weybridge and its environs to pick up the Wey Navigation Canal at New Haw. We follow the canal to Weybridge and the Wey and Thames back to Walton. The walking is easy and flat, although there is the usual towpath mud after wet weather, and there is much of interest to see on the water and banks of the various rivers.

Station: Weybridge (SR from Waterloo). Pick up the walk at (A).
Bus: 218 (Kingston to Staines). Stop nearest Walton Bridge.
Car park: Immediately after crossing Walton Bridge on the A244 towards Walton turn right on a small road leading down to the riverside and a large car park on the left.
Refreshments: In Weybridge and New Haw.

From the car park near Walton Bridge cross the road to the riverside path and turn left. On reaching a bridge, an extension of just under a mile can be made by crossing to the island and following the towpath. At first numerous rugby pitches are passed on the left and then the church and picturesque houses and cottages at Shepperton come into view on the opposite bank. This island is designated a Surrey Open Space and is a very unspoilt and beautiful spot. If you wish to bypass the island (which can be visited on the return journey), continue along the towpath past Desborough Cut and another bridge (toilets near here) and on towards Shepperton Lock and weir. The island just before the weir with the footbridge across it is D'Oyly Carte Island, once the home of Richard D'Oyly Carte. There is now a ferry service to Shepperton which runs half hourly at weekends and hourly on weekdays. The weir is very impressive after heavy rain and canoeists are often seen battling against the white water. Continue to the end of the towpath and then follow the road past several inns to emerge at the centre of Weybridge.

Cross the road to the column erected to the memory of Fredericka, Duchess of York, who for thirty years lived at Oatlands, near Weybridge. Take the small road opposite the column; it soon narrows to a passage between houses. At the busy road ahead turn left and cross the road to take the first turning on the right, Springfield Meadows. At the recreation ground the path runs along the left-hand edge, with a good view of Weybridge church on the right. Go past a path coming in on the left and at a crossing track, with the path leading from the church, turn left towards a road. Cross this and turn right for a short distance to a turning on the left. Go down here to a road on the right, Windsor Walk. When this road bends to the left, go straight ahead on a gravelly road. About 30 yards after a lamp post on the right, turn right along a footpath leading through a wood to the railway line. Follow the path by the line towards Weybridge station.

(A) Cross the bridge to the south side, and turn right through the car park of the station. Continue on a path by the side of the railway which leads out to a small road. After an electricity substation, cross a bridge over the line and turn left to follow the asphalted path. After crossing the river Wey on a footbridge, continue on to a picturesque pond with marked pegs for the fishermen. At the end of the pond, turn off right to

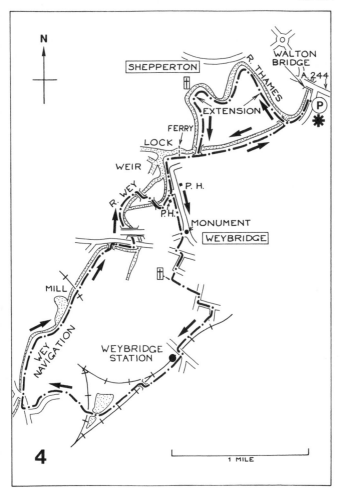

take a path running between this pond and a smaller one on the left.

Go up over another railway line and go forward on a pleasant path between fields, later passing a public footpath sign on the left. When the path ahead bends to the left past houses, take the marked footpath by the side of a field. When this emerges at a main road, cross left to the road opposite. This leads to the lock at New Haw. Do not cross the river but go over the road and follow the towpath by the side of the Wey Navigation Canal for about two miles.

About half way along the towpath there is a large mill on the left with its millpond and lock and weir which has been recently renovated and converted into flats. Go under the railway bridge and follow the towpath to a bridge. Cross this and take the path going in the same direction as before but now on the other side of the canal. On coming to a lock, cross the main road *before* the river bridge into Weybridge and take the path over a small brick bridge ahead and in 30 yards bear right to the river. Turn left under the bridge and follow the towpath by the side of the river Wey until it finishes by a small lock and cottage. Go over the steep little footbridge and continue forward on an enclosed concrete path. Go over a small road to cross the iron footbridge ahead. Turn left down a series of passages (Church Walk) which leads past an old inn to the road. Turn left back to the towpath at the weir and Shepperton Lock. Retrace your steps back to the car park at Walton Bridge.

(N.B. Those who started the walk from Weybridge station can either turn left at the inn to go along the towpath to the bridge crossing to the island and follow the path round the island and back along the towpath, or for a shorter walk, turn right to pick up the walk at the column in the centre of Weybridge.)

5. Bushy Park, Hampton Court and Home Park

Distance: 5¹/₂ miles
Grid reference: 153702.
Ordnance Survey maps: 1:50,000 sheet 176; 1:25,000 sheet TQ 06/16.

Hampton Court, built by Cardinal Wolsey over four hundred years ago and later annexed by Henry VIII, is the focal point of this walk but there are also many other interesting features to see. The Woodland Gardens in Bushy Park are a particular delight in early spring when the daffodils are in bloom and later on the azaleas, rhododendrons, camellias and heathers present a colourful display. Water is never far away in this walk and we pass many lakes, ponds, streams and the Thames.

Station: Hampton Court (SR from Waterloo). From the station turn right over Hampton Court Bridge and follow the wall of the palace to the Lion Gates, to join the walk by the signpost inside the gates [marked at paragraph (A)].
Buses: 111, 131, 216, Green Line 715, 716, 718, 726: stop near the Lion Gates (join walk at A). 201, 267: stop near the roundabout (cross to the main entrance of the palace and turn left to follow the outside wall round to the Lion Gates).
Car park: In Bushy Park opposite Bushy House. From Teddington go down the Main Avenue in Bushy Park and take the first turning right.
Refreshments: In Hampton Court Palace in the Tilt Yard, and cafes in Hampton Court Road.

Bushy Park comprises 1,100 acres (445 hectares) and the central avenue of chestnut trees was originally planned by Sir Christopher Wren as part of his grand design for William III's alterations to Hampton Court. The trees are a gorgeous sight when they are in bloom and on Chestnut Sunday, which is about the middle of May, many visitors come to see the beautiful display. Herds of deer graze peacefully in the park and visitors should not feed them. Bushy House, first built in the reign of Charles II, was rebuilt in the early eighteenth century. It was for long occupied by the Rangers of Bushy Park, who included the Earl of Halifax, Lord North and William IV (while Duke of Clarence). William lived here with Dorothy Jordan, the actress, by whom he had nine children. The house was converted for use by the National Physical Laboratory, which opened here in 1902 for scientific and industrial research. The upper floors of the house are now for the personal use of the Director of the Laboratory.

At the end of the car park nearest to Bushy House, take the grassy path leading away diagonally left towards the fence and entrance gate of the plantation. It should be noted that the gates are closed at dusk. Enter the plantation and go forward to cross a small bridge linking two ponds. There are many varieties of ducks and geese to be seen here and also some fine black swans.

Turn right at the crossing track past the bridge and follow the path through the plantation. Leave by the gate and cross the horse ride to enter the Woodland Gardens at another gate. Pass a small turning off to the left and at a fork keep left (at rhododendron time it is worth going right to see some of the magnificent blooms). At a T junction turn right under an arch made by a shrub, then first left over a wooden bridge. After a few yards, bear right on a path through rhododendrons. On reaching the main path by a small waterfall, turn left and then immediately take the path leading up past some seats overlooking the pond fringed by willows. Follow the path down by the stream to turn off left, just before an exit, on a green sward with large trees. In azalea time the reflections on the water on the right are superb. Go over a small footbridge across a trickle of water and turn right towards another bridge. After crossing this, turn left towards an extensive heather garden, which is a comparatively recent addition to these beautifully kept gardens. Go left round the far side of a tranquil pool and then right over another bridge, ignore a left turning and at a T junction turn right out through a gate. Turn right towards the brick bridge at the end of the fences to the plantations. Follow the grassy path along the left-hand side of the Longford river and at the end of the water bear half-right across the grass under the trees towards the entrance gates to Bushy Park, keeping the road on the left, and passing the Diana Fountain on the left. This statue (*circa* 1640) is now thought to depict Venus. Cross the busy main road by the pedestrian crossing to enter Hampton Court through the Lion Gates. (For the station and buses turn right and follow the road round to the station and bus stops.)

(A) At the signpost ahead, take the path half-left leading towards the Vine and the Mantegna Paintings Exhibition. Go through the green wooden gates out to the Broad Walk, with its lavishly laid-out flower beds and wide herbaceous border, always a mass of colour in season. Turn right towards the palace.

At the east front of the palace a diversion can be made by turning right at the end of the palace to visit the Pond Garden, the Knot Garden with its aromatic herbs and the Great Vine, planted in 1768, with its main stem of nearly 80 inches (2 metres) in girth. If often yields a crop of as many as five or six hundred bunches of black grapes, which are on sale. At the east front turn left towards the fountain in the circular pond and skirt the pond to the statuary by the iron railings. Turn right to cross the bridge and go through the magnificent wrought iron gates into the Home Park. Turn left towards the Long Water and continue along the edge to the end. Cross the road and take the metalled track ahead leading past a pond used by model boat enthusiasts. Go right on a grassy path to skirt the edge of the pond past a seat to a gate in the fence by a notice board. Go down the wide track between fences out to the towpath by the Thames.

Turn left past Ravens Ait, used for instructing young people in canoeing and sailing, and continue on the towpath for about a mile towards Kingston Bridge, built from 1825 to 1828. This path, known as Barge Walk, leads out to the main road. Turn left down to the roundabout and keep left to cross over the road by the pedestrian crossing to Kingston Bridge House. Go left, then right down Church Grove and in about 100 yards go through the metal gate opposite the church. Go down this tree-lined path by the recreation ground to a gate

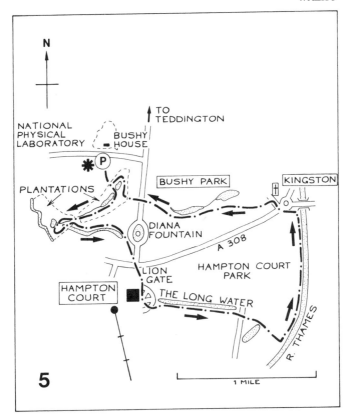

at the end. Continue on the grassy path to the end of the wooden fence on the right and at the corner of the fence take the path ahead, i.e. the third track from the right. Keep on this path over several crossing tracks, passing a wood of oak and pine trees on the right. At the large pond ahead, keep along its left-hand bank towards a large car park. Just before the car park, cross a small planked bridge on the right and continue in the same direction. At the end of a stream on the right, turn left past a water pump towards the road. Cross the road to a metalled track opposite, signposted 'No admittance for unauthorised vehicles'. About 50 yards before the fence ahead, turn left on a rough path which leads over a stream and turn right to the gate leading into the planta-

21

tion. (Should the plantation be closed, follow the fence of the plantation on your left to the road leading to the car park.) In the plantation,
cross the bridge on the right and follow the path round the edge, to
leave by the gate through which you entered and cross the grass back to
the car park. For the station and buses, continue from the beginning of
the walk at the entrance gate to the plantation.

6. Osterley Park and the Grand Union Canal

Distance: 5^1/$_2$ miles (6^1/$_2$ from station and buses).
Grid reference: 147779.
Ordnance Survey maps: 1:50,000 sheet 176; 1:25,000 sheet TQ 07/
17.

*This walk explores the lakes and grounds of Osterley Park with the
opportunity of visiting Osterley House. The original manor house was
built in the sixteenth century by Sir Thomas Gresham and Queen Elizabeth visited it in 1576. The old house was encased in new walls in the
mid eighteenth century and Robert Adam was responsible for much of
the design and the interior decoration. The stables are only slightly
altered since Gresham's day. The house (NT) is open daily, excluding
Mondays, Good Friday and 24-27 December, 11 a.m. to 5 p.m. There
is an entrance fee. The walk continues across fields to Norwood Green
and then to the Grand Union Canal for an interesting section with five
locks set close together. We return to Osterley Park via the larger of
the two lakes.*

Buses: 91, 116. Stop on A4 (Great West Road) near Osterley Park.
Station: Osterley (LT, Piccadilly Line). From the station turn left and
then first left up to the entrance gates of Osterley Park. Walk through
the park up to the car park on the left.
Car park: In the grounds of Osterley Park (free) or park in side roads.
Refreshments: Tea room open March to end October in Osterley Park.
Inns in Norwood Green and along the Grand Union Canal.

From the car park in Osterley Park, take the path leading to the lake
on the left and walk along beside the lake, soon passing a tree enclosed
by railings. The attractive lake has many interesting species of geese

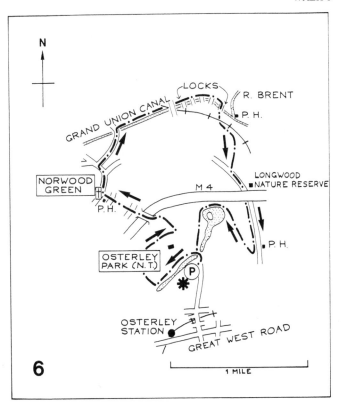

and ducks. At the end of the lake, go up to a brick bridge on the left and bear right on a path leading round the grounds of the house, eventually passing a summer house on the right with an ornamental ceiling. There is a fine group of cedars here. Go out of the gate into the parkland, with cattle grazing, and turn left towards the lodge gates. Go through the lodges and turn left to cross over the M4. Go down steps ahead and cross the field to a row of houses ahead. Go between the houses and cross the road to a passage leading out to Norwood Green by the Plough inn.

Turn right and go round the bend to take the first turning on the left. Turn first right and at the end of this avenue cross the narrow bridge by Norwood Top Lock. Go left on the towpath and then left again under

23

the bridge. The next bridge over the Grand Union Canal is a road bridge and underneath the canal is the railway line, giving an unusual and slightly eerie three-tier effect. Next comes Hanwell Lock, a series of five locks set close together, climbing a steep gradient and looking very impressive from the bottom. At the last of these five, cross the lock to follow a footpath sign to Osterley. (If you wish to visit the Fox inn, which is a short way further on, do not cross the lock but continue on over the bridge across the Brent river and turn left.)

Go past a notice about the landscaping of the land in the Brent River Park to commemorate the Queen's Silver Jubilee. Cross a field to a stile by the railway line. On the other side of the line turn left to follow the narrow path between the mesh fence bordering huge playing fields and the railway track. (If this narrow path is overgrown, you need not cross the railway line but turn left through a field and keep near the line to cross it further on to rejoin the path at the right-angled bend.) Follow the path round a right-angled bend still keeping the sports ground on the right, out to the main road. Turn left to the motorway. (There is a pleasant optional diversion on the left here to Longwood Nature Reserve.) Go under the motorway up to the Hare and Hounds inn on the left. Cross the road and follow the footpath, with the hedge and wall on the right.

At the lodges to Osterley Park, turn right on the drive between fields and when you get near the M4 go through a gate in the fence on the left leading to a pretty path near the lake. At the end of this part of the extensive lake, you can either cross the grass towards the house or follow the banks of the lake past the islands back to the bridge between the two lakes and the car park.

7. Twickenham riverside, Richmond Park and Marble Hill

Distance: 6¹/₂ miles or 5 miles.
Grid reference: 175738.
Ordnance Survey maps: 1:50,000 sheet 176; 1:25,000 sheet TQ 07/
17.

*This is a walk of considerable interest and variety within a compara-
tively short distance. After leaving Marble Hill with its Palladian
villa, we explore the riverside at Twickenham with its many fascinating*

houses, cottages and the famous Eel Pie Island. We then take the towpath into Richmond and walk along the opposite bank to the Terrace Gardens, past the renowned view on Richmond Hill and into Richmond Park. The walk can be extended here to take in one of the woodland plantations. We leave the park to descend into Petersham and walk back along the river into Richmond and thence to Twickenham.

Station: St Margarets (SR from Waterloo). Turn right past a road to go down Crown Road and cross the A306. Turn left to an entrance into Marble Hill on the right. Marble Hill House is clearly visible ahead. This adds about a mile to the walk altogether.

Buses: 33, 90B, 202, R70. Stop on A306 by entrance to Marble Hill in Twickenham.

Car park: In Marble Hill Park. Entrance in railings just before the Rising Sun Steak House on the corner of A306. (Closes at dusk.)

Refreshments: Numerous snack bars and cafes (not always open in the winter) and pubs along the route. Pembroke Lodge in Richmond Park, closed Monday to Friday from November to January but open during weekend; open daily from February to October.

From the car park in Marble Hill walk across the grass to the cream facade of Marble Hill House, a Palladian villa built during 1723-9 for the Countess of Suffolk, mistress of George II. The house is open to the public on weekdays 10 a.m. to 6 p.m. (10 a.m. to 4 p.m., October to end of February). There is no admission charge. Go past the house and the fenced enclosure where young children can play; on the right is the stable block and a small cafe (open weekends from 10 a.m. to 4 p.m. in the winter and more frequently in the summer). The large house on the right just past the stable block was once owned by the poet Walter de la Mare. At the exit to the park, you may wish to see Montpelier Row, described by Pevsner as 'one of the best examples near London of a well mannered, well proportioned terrace development'. If so, turn right and then right again into Chapel Road. Number 15 Montpelier Row was owned by Tennyson from 1851 to 1853.

Having seen Montpelier Row, retrace your steps past the gate to the park and after a few yards turn right through an archway into the woodland garden which adjoins Orleans Gallery and the Octagon room, built in 1720. Take the left fork through the woodland. The gallery is away to the right and is opened to the public at certain times, free of charge, by the local authority. Many exhibitions and art displays are held here, and the times of opening are displayed at the entrance. The Octagon Room is used for concerts and other events and is to one side of the gallery.

At the exit to the woodland garden and the gallery, turn right down the small road known as Riverside. Be careful of cars here as there is no pavement and there are some sharp bends. Twickenham Ferry (recently closed) was in existence from the mid-seventeenth century and provided a useful short cut to Ham House. There is a ferry to Ham House at Hammertons, which is passed later in the walk. After passing the quaint White Swan inn, with its terrace and riverside garden, turn right up Sion Road, where there is an exquisite terrace of houses built in 1721, known as Sion Row. Turn left into the gardens of York House by the tennis courts. At the greenhouse, turn left to some very attractive gardens and go up some steps on the right past a Japanese garden. York House on the right is now municipal offices but was once owned by the Duc d'Orleans and later became the home of Sir Ratan J. Tata, an Indian merchant prince. Go over the stone footbridge leading to the riverside section of the gardens and turn right by the goldfish pond towards the startling statuary group which was brought from Italy by Sir Ratan Tata. This group of maidens diving for pearls has been restored recently, and the waterfall is now operational for the first time for many years. The terrace by the river overlooks Eel Pie Island, a famous pleasure resort in the nineteenth century and visited by the Prince Regent in his youth. Richmond Park can be seen in the distance on the left.

Return over the bridge to York House and turn right down the steps. Turn left towards the house and then right to the tennis courts. Turn left alongside the courts and out to the road leading to the main entrance. Turn left and then right which leads to a new complex of municipal offices and a day centre for the elderly. Turn left down the new road towards St Mary's church. At the church the road ahead was once the main thoroughfare through Twickenham. Turn left past the church and in 20 yards go right towards the car park. In another 20 yards turn left to the river, passing the Mary Wallace Theatre on the left and the Barmy Arms inn on the right which was established in 1727. Eel Pie Island is opposite. Turn left and then left again to take some steps up on the right to pass the churchyard, where Alexander Pope is buried. Dial House on the left was long associated with the Twining family and is now the vicarage. A new sundial on the front of the house has recently replaced a very old one. Continue along the road under the bridge from York House back to Orleans Gardens on the right. Go up the shallow steps towards the river and follow the towpath to Richmond Bridge. Ham House, which is visited in Walk 9, can be seen across the river and Hammerton's ferry to Ham House is here. At the entrance to Marble Hill, the large tree surrounded by railings is a black walnut planted in the early nineteenth century and reputed to be the largest in Britain.

After passing Richmond Ice Rink, cross Richmond Bridge and go

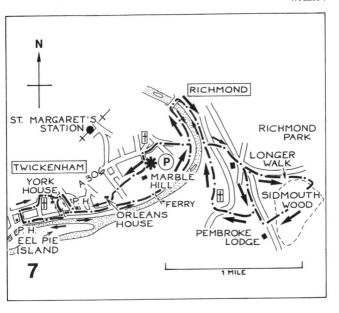

N

ST. MARGARET'S
STATION

RICHMOND

RICHMOND
PARK

TWICKENHAM

LONGER
WALK

YORK
HOUSE

A 305

MARBLE
HILL

SIDMOUTH
WOOD

P. H.

FERRY

ORLEANS
HOUSE

P. H.
EEL PIE
ISLAND

PEMBROKE
LODGE

7

1 MILE

down the steps on the right to the Riverside Gardens. This is a very popular part in the summer and is usually thronged with visitors. After some way along the towpath, just past the Three Pigeons inn, cross the Petersham Road to the Terrace Gardens by means of the subway with a grotto-like entrance. The Terrace Gardens were opened to the public in 1887 by the Duchess of Teck, great-grandmother of Queen Elizabeth II. Open-air productions of Shakespeare's plays are held here in the summer. Go up the path towards the cafe and follow the path round to the right (you can make a more extensive circuit of the gardens by turning left before the cafe). Go through an archway on the right to take the path across the rough grass towards the Star and Garter Home ahead. Climb the steps with white railings up to the viewpoint at Terrace Walk, from which there is a celebrated view across the Thames valley. Open-air art exhibitions are sometimes held on this wide terrace.

The conspicuous nineteenth-century building below the terrace is now the Petersham Hotel. Continue towards the Star and Garter Home, passing the elegant house known as The Wick, built in 1775, and also Wick House, built for Sir Joshua Reynolds in 1772, and now used as a nurses' hostel for the staff of the Star and Garter Home. The Home itself, for disabled servicemen, is an imposing building facing the entrance to the park and opened in 1924.

Cross the road to enter Richmond Park, which occupies an area of 2,400 acres (970 hectares) and was first enclosed in 1637 by Charles I. (For an extension of about 1¹/₂ miles, continue ahead past the roundabout, on the grass verge by the road leading to Roehampton Gate. Follow the fence of the plantation on the right round to a gate. There are fine views here across to Pen Ponds and White Lodge. Go through the pleasant woodland to leave the plantation by another gate. Pembroke Lodge cafe and restaurant are a short distance away to the left. Cross the road and turn right past King Harry's Mound, a prehistoric barrow, and follow the fence to a gate.)

If you do not wish to go on the extension, turn right inside the park past the toilets and follow the hedgerow path to an iron gate.

All walkers now go through the gate and pass a memorial to James Thompson on the right. After going through a laburnum walk, branch left and then right up to the seats and sundial on King Harry's Mound. It is reputed that Henry VIII watched from here to see a signal from Windsor Castle that Anne Boleyn had been beheaded at the Tower of London. At the back of this mound there is a gap in the hedge through which St Paul's Cathedral is visible on a clear day, as if through a telescope. From the mound, follow the path down to a padlocked gate into the park and bend sharply right past the foot of the mound towards a gate on the left leading into Petersham Park.

Go through the gate (another magnificent view from here across the Thames valley) and follow the path leading down diagonally right across Petersham Park. Leave the park by the iron gates at the bottom and turn left along the Petersham Road. Just before a sharp corner, cross the road to take a small lane leading past the tiny parish church of St Peter, where George Vancouver lies buried. He was an explorer with Captain Cook and circumnavigated the world. Vancouver in British Columbia is named after him and, when St Peter's was damaged during the war, donations were sent from British Columbia to help towards repairing the damage. When the lane bends round to the left to some nurseries, continue forward on a path between hedges through Petersham meadows, a peaceful scene with the cows grazing. Go through the railings at the end of the path and cross the field to join the towpath back to Richmond Bridge. Cross back to the Twickenham side and go down the steps to cross the slipway (if not flooded) and follow the towpath back past the ice rink. Turn right down Cambridge Park footpath at the end of a brick wall by a notice prohibiting bicycles. Keep forward down the road when the passage ends. Turn left down Cambridge Park (numbers 15-21) to come out on the main road with the Rising Sun public house opposite and St Stephen's church on the right. Enter Marble Hill Park for the car park. Retrace your steps back to Crown Road on the right for the station at St Margarets.

8.   Kew Gardens and the towpath to Richmond

Distance: 5¹/₂ miles (7 from station).
Grid reference: 187760.
Ordnance Survey maps: 1:50,000 sheet 176; 1:25,000 sheet TQ 07/17.

This walk is centred in the Royal Botanic Gardens at Kew (no dogs allowed), which cover an area of approximately 300 acres (120 hectares) and which originate from the private botanic garden initiated by Princess Augusta, mother of George III, in the grounds of Kew House. The suggested route covers many of the best known features in the gardens but may be deviated from to see other seasonal attractions. The walk leaves by the Brentford Gate to take the towpath to Richmond and crosses Richmond Green to return to Kew.

Buses: 27, 65. Stop outside the Lion Gate.
Station: Kew Gardens: LT (District Line); BR Broad Street to Richmond. Go down Lichfield Road and enter Kew Gardens by Victoria Gate. Turn left down the path to the Lion Gate. This adds about 1¹/₂ miles to the walk, although it is possible to get the 90B bus back to the station from Richmond.
Car park: Park in Lion Park Gate Gardens opposite the Lion Gate, or in one of the other side turnings on the right.
Refreshments: In Kew Gardens, tea pavilion (closed in winter) and tea bar near Brentford Gate. Also in Richmond.

Enter Kew Gardens by the Lion Gate (admission charge) and go ahead. Just past the kiosk and notice board, down the avenue on the right, you will see a dovecote with some beautiful white fan-tailed pigeons. They are very tame and call to each other with a soft cooing sound.

Do not go down this avenue but continue ahead with the golf course on the left, passing the heather garden on the right and soon coming to the Pagoda. This was erected in 1761-2 and is ten storeys high, each storey being one foot shorter than the one below. Its appearance was

29

once more spectacular as each angle of the roof was decorated with a guardian dragon covered in a film of multicoloured glass, which produced a dazzling reflection. The Pagoda is not considered safe enough to open to the public.

After passing the azalea beds, turn right on the metalled track to the Japanese Gateway on the right. This is a replica, four-fifths of the size of the original, of a famous Japanese gate, the Gate of the Imperial Messenger in Kyoto. It was presented to the gardens after being shown at the Japanese-British Exhibition of 1910. Note the netting over the roof to protect it from birds picking out the thatch. Cross over the first crossing track, which leads down to the refreshment pavilion on the right (open in summer), and at the next slanted crossing track, with 'sleeping policemen' (humps in the path), turn right towards the large Temperate House and the Australian House. After passing the Temperate House on the right, bend round to the right to the entrance and then go left down an avenue of trees, some of whose branches trail on the ground creating little rooms. Go up the steps at the end of the avenue and fork left past King William's Temple. Go over a crossing track and past a fine group of cedars on the right, making for the 120 yard long Palm House designed by Decimus Burton. At the Rose Garden, turn right past the Palm House to the pond. The Queen's Beasts paraded outside the Palm House are stone copies of plaster originals which were placed outside the annex to Westminster Abbey at the Coronation in 1953. Go past the pond and turn right up to a round bed with a Grecian urn at a junction of paths. Take the middle path, i.e. straight ahead, which leads to a T junction. Bear left, passing the woodland garden on the right. This path leads to the Princess of Wales Conservatory. Just past the entrance, bear right at a fork and take the first turning on the left into the Rock Garden. You will see the Temple of Aeolus atop the mound on the right. In the Rock Garden turn left to wander through this beautifully landscaped area, complete with trickling water. Keep on the main path and at the second fork, with steps to the right, continue on to skirt the pond on the right and emerge from the garden. At the cross paths the Alpine House and Aquatic Garden are on the right. We turn left, however, past the Princess of Wales Conservatory once more. At the T junction turn right and at the crossing track turn left to go past the Orangery (bookstall and exhibition). At the Broad Walk ahead, turn right and then left towards Kew Palace and its interesting herb garden. Kew Palace, or the Dutch House as it is sometimes called, was built in 1631 and became the King's residence in 1803 when the original Kew Palace was destroyed. It contains souvenirs of George III and his family and is open to the public in the summer. Go to the left of the Palace through the Queen's garden and up to the black and gold summer

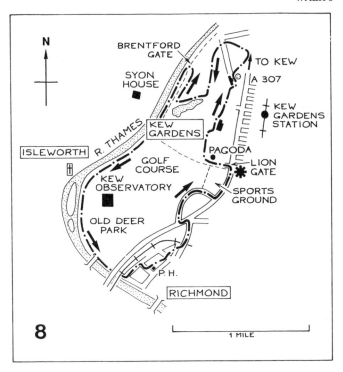

house on top of a mound. Follow the path near the river towards the new Sir Joseph Banks building set in lakeland surroundings. An audio-visual show is given in the basement every half an hour.

Continue on to the wide path leading to the Main Gate and turn right, passing the Filmy Fern house on the left. Turn left on to the Broad Walk and first right. Continue on this path past several crossing tracks to just before a junction of tracks with a signpost to the Bamboo Garden, *et cetera* and the Palm House visible on the left. Turn right and bear left across the grass to the lake. Keep on the right-hand side of the lake, passing a landing stage formed by granite blocks which were once part of London Bridge (1831-1967). At the end of the lake there is a fine view across to Syon House on the other side of the river. Walk towards Syon House and just before the towpath turn right on a path which leads into the Rhododendron Dell, planted about 1773 by 'Capability' Brown. Just before the end of the dell, turn left and at a T

31

junction turn right. Keep left at a fork to go towards the Brentford Gate. The tea bar is about 100 yards round to the right.

Leave Kew Gardens by the Brentford Gate and turn left along the towpath, soon passing Syon House again, the seat of the Duke of Northumberland. The obelisk we go past on the left inside Old Deer Park was one of three set up as meridian marks which were used to provide London's official time before Greenwich mean time was adopted. Kew Observatory, built in 1769 for George III, is situated in the park and was used by the Meteorological Office until it was closed recently. On the opposite bank, just before the island, is a quaint group of buildings. The church was built in 1967 after a fire destroyed the one in 1943. It has an unusual vaulted roof and tall windows. A church has stood on this site since AD 695 and it is said that Henry VIII's body rested there on his last journey up the Thames. The London Apprentice pub and restaurant are very popular and the houses opposite present a colourful scene. The wharf further upstream lies on the Duke of Northumberland River, which was constructed in the fifteenth century. Mills here were used in the making of gunpowder until the 1920s, and, until the end of the nineteenth century, in the manufacture of swords, brass, copper and paper.

Just past the footbridge and lock at Isleworth (the lowest lock on the Thames) there is a small bridge on the left crossing to the Old Deer Park. Continue on the towpath under the Twickenham road bridge and the railway bridge. The view here has been a favourite subject for many painters. In the centre is Richmond Bridge and in the background is Richmond Hill. On the left is Asgill House, built in 1758 for Sir Charles Asgill, Lord Mayor of London. Turn left up Palace Lane, past a notice on the wall giving some information about the old Richmond Palace, formerly the Palace of Shene. The White Swan inn and the row of cottages present a delightful picture. On coming to Richmond Green, the scene of tournaments in Tudor times, go past some beautiful houses on the right to Old Palace Yard. Very little remains of the old palace but the building on the left is the Wardrobe, which was formerly the household offices of the palace. It has been extensively reconstructed but retains some of the original brickwork and timbers. One gateway still survives and there is a plaque by the arch bearing the arms of Henry VII. The next group of houses by the green is Maids of Honour Row. Cross the green on the path by the cricket ground with the Cricketers inn on the right. Cricket has been played here since the 1600s. There are some delightful alleys leading down to the main street in Richmond, with many fascinating antique shops and jewellers. Cross the road to Little Green, with the ornate Richmond Theatre on the right. Go over the narrow railway bridge and down Parkshot Road. The new Richmond Court House on the left occupies the site of

a house where George Eliot lived in 1855-69 while she was writing
Adam Bed. (Richmond station is reached by a cutting by the railway
line, and buses back to Lion Gate and the 90B to Kew Gardens station
are available opposite the station.)

At the main road, cross to Kew Foot Road opposite, either by the
traffic lights (110 yards to the right) or the footbridge (250 yards left).
Go past the golf driving range and Richmond Hospital and continue
forward down an alley to a residential road; turn right to the main road.
Go left, past the rugby ground on the left, back to Lion Gate.

9. Richmond Park and Ham Common

Distance: 6½ miles or 4 miles.
Grid reference: 214724.
Ordnance Survey maps: 1:50,000 sheet 176; 1:25,000 sheets TQ 07/
17 and TQ 27/37.

*A fine walk through Richmond Park to the Isabella Plantation, which
is at its best when the azaleas and rhododendrons are flowering in
April and May, but at weekends there can be long queues at the car
parks at this time. We leave the park by Ham Gate, crossing Ham
common to visit Ham House, once the home of Earls of Dysart and
now a National Trust property (open daily, except Mondays, 11 a.m. to
5.30 p.m.). After a short walk along by the Thames we turn into
Petersham and back to Richmond Park, passing Pen Ponds on the way
to Robin Hood Gate. The shorter walk does not leave Richmond Park.*

Bus: 85 (Putney Bridge to Kingston); Green Line 715, 718. Stop
nearest to Robin Hood Gate.
Car park: By Robin Hood Gate in Richmond Park. (No exit from the
park by this gate.) The park closes at dusk.
Refreshments: Inns at Ham and Petersham. Pembroke Lodge in Richmond Park, open during weekends only from November to January,
open daily from February to October.

From the car park in Richmond Park near Robin Hood Gate, cross
the road by the small roundabout in the park and go forward, keeping
close to the road signposted to Pen Ponds. Just before the road bends
to the right, there is a small pond on the left-hand side, called Martin's
Pond. Go round the top of the pond, cross the horse track and take the
right-hand grassy path, which leads slightly uphill towards a fenced

wood named Prince Charles's Spinney. At the fence keep right for a
short distance to cross a stile into the plantation. Follow this wide
fenced path to the far side of the plantation. Look out for green
woodpeckers and jays amongst many other birds in this lovely peaceful woodland.

After climbing the stile to leave the spinney, turn right and follow
the fence to the corner. Cross a wide track to go forward on a small
path. At the next crossing track turn left and keep to the right fork
almost immediately. This path leads towards the Isabella Plantation on
the right. Continue forward at some white posts and follow the plantation fence to the gate. Once inside, there are various paths to follow by
streams and over bridges. Go through the plantation to leave by the
main exit near an attractive pond by the heather garden. Cross the
small car park for disabled drivers and, when the track bends to the
right, fork left on a grassy path leading to a junction of roads with a
white notice.

For the shorter walk, cross the road, continue forward and then turn
right and walk along the escarpment to pick up the walk again at
Pembroke Lodge.

For the longer walk, cross the road and continue forward on a path
above the road leading to Ham Gate. At a junction take the middle
path. Descend the slope to a large pond at the entrance to the park
(toilets here). Leave the park by Ham Gate and pass a large house on
the left. At the edge of Ham Common on the left, take a path leading
diagonally left on to the common (marked as a horse ride). There are
many paths criss-crossing this commonland but if you keep near the
horse ride this leads through the middle and, after about half a mile,
emerges near the crossroads with a notice to Ham House opposite. The
New Inn is on the right. Go down the road opposite, by the side of the
green, and, shortly after Martingales Close on the right, turn right to go
through a gap in some palings and take a wide path between
fences with a fine vista of Ham House in the distance.

Cross a road and continue forward to the iron gates to Ham House.
Swing round to the right and at the end of the wall to the house, turn
left down the metalled track. Ham polo grounds are on the right. This
track leads down to a barrier with the entrance to Ham House on the
left. Ham House dates from 1610 and contains many interesting an-
tiques and treasures. To reach the towpath, go slightly right by the side
of a field and through a gap in the hedge. In winter there is a fine view
of Marble Hill House across the river; this is visited in Walk 7.

Turn right along the towpath for about a quarter of a mile and,
opposite an island, turn right up River Lane. On reaching the Petersham Road, turn left past The Dysarts. Cross the road to enter Petersham
Park through a metal gate at the end of some iron railings. Take the

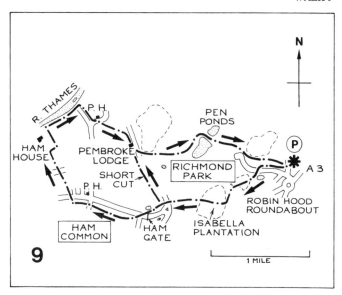

wide path on the left going uphill, passing a clump of cedars and conifers on the left. (Do not take the path bending sharply left by the wall of the park.) Go through the gate at the top of the rise into Richmond Park. There is a magnificent view from the top overlooking the Thames valley. Go up the shallow steps on the right and turn right along the path through the formal gardens leading towards Pembroke Lodge restaurant and cafeteria. Pembroke Lodge dates from about 1800 and was granted by Queen Victoria to her prime minister, Lord John Russell, whose grandson, Bertrand Russell, spent much of his boyhood here.

Both walks continue here. Go through the gates past the toilets into the car park and cross the road to a track leading past the right-hand corner of the plantation opposite. Follow the fence on the left across a tarmac track and then go half-right away from the fence with a pond off to the far right. Cross a road leading to a house and continue forward, passing the house on the left, on the track nearest to the house which leads easterly to Pen Ponds ahead, with the tall Roehampton flats behind. Cross over several tracks and just before the larger of the Pen Ponds, join a sandy track running beside the banks of the pond. At the end turn right across the causeway between the two ponds. Ice skating is popular on these ponds when the ice is considered to be thick

enough. Continue forward past the car park and cross the road. Keep
on up towards the brow of Spankers Hill Wood and follow the path on
the escarpment. When this bends round to the left, take the grassy path
ahead leading down to the car park at Robin Hood Gate.

10. Wimbledon Common, Putney Heath and Richmond Park

Distance: 6¹/₂ miles or 4 miles.
Grid reference: 214724.
Ordnance Survey maps: 1:50,000 sheet 176; 1:25,000 sheet TQ 27/37.

*Wimbledon Common, with its windmill, is said to have been a favourite
haunt of duellists long ago, and Caesar's Camp, an iron age encamp-
ment of 14 acres (6 hectares), is combined with part of Putney Heath
and Richmond Park to make an interesting walk of about 6¹/₂ miles. A
shorter walk of 4 miles based solely on Wimbledon Common is also
included.*

Bus: 85 (Putney Bridge to Kingston); Green Line 715, 718. Stop
nearest to Robin Hood Gate.
Car park: By Robin Hood Gate in Richmond Park. (No exit from the
park by this gate.) The park closes at dusk.
Refreshments: Windmill Tea Rooms on Wimbledon Common. Inn at
Roehampton on longer walk.

After parking the car in the car park near Robin Hood Gate, cross the
busy main road at Robin Hood roundabout to a horse barrier opposite.
Go under the barrier, turn half-left and after 50 yards fork right to a gap
in the trees by a small stream. Cross a rough field and keep to the left-
hand side of playing fields to make for a wooden bridge on the left.
Cross over Beverley Brook, turn right and follow the river for just over
a mile, passing a bridge on the right and several paths off to the left. At
the second footbridge, with playing fields on the other side of the river,
turn sharp left and follow the grassy path through some trees to some
posts. Keep on slightly uphill on a stony path bordered by a narrow
belt of trees. Continue on up to a wire fence and cross a path to carry
on uphill on a path running through a golf course.

Towards the top of the rise there is a low stone on the left which
marks one of the borders of the Rounds (or Caesar's Camp). The next

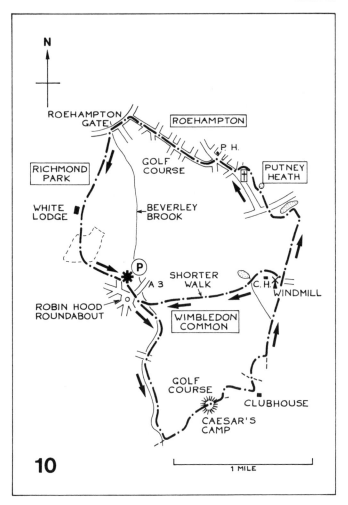

stone is some 300 yards further on and there is a plaque by the side of it, which is somewhat defaced, but says 'An iron age fort probably in the third century BC. The fort was surrounded by a circular earthwork about 300 yards in diameter and two ramparts with a ditch between them...' The camp is well placed with fine views.

At a lane, shortly after the stone, turn left down a road signposted to Warren Farm. After 175 yards, turn right into woodland on a path marked by white concrete posts near a second bend to the left in the lane. Keep ahead on a definite path through the trees leading up to the golf course. This path emerges from the wood with mounds ahead. The club house is away to the right. Keep forward half-left to an unmade-up track leading to the club house and turn right towards the car park.

Just before the car park, turn left and continue forward over a crossing track, past a seat inscribed 'Enid, Joe and Shandy' and then a golf green on the right. Cross over a fairway and keep on in a northerly direction to reach a horse ride. Turn right up to a signpost marked 'Authorised Vehicles Only' by a road and turn left to follow a small path by the side of the road. This leads to the windmill and the club house of the Anglo-Scottish Golf Club. The windmill is a combined smock and post mill and is marked by a plaque saying that Lord Baden-Powell once lived in the house below the windmill and wrote *Scouting for Boys* there. There is also a small museum open weekend afternoons and Bank Holidays from April to October. Just round the corner from the windmill are some excellent tea rooms.

For the shorter walk (4 miles)

Circle the windmill and club house to a corner of the fence by the club house facing one of the fairways. Take the path down a gully through the trees. At the small lake called Queen's Mere, take the second path on the left uphill. Cross over one of the fairways (taking care when golfers are around) and take the right fork. At a junction of about four paths, continue forward in the same direction over another fairway and downhill through a wood, passing a single beech tree on the left. At a slanting T junction, turn right towards the war memorial. Go through the enclosure surrounding the memorial and on reaching the playing fields either go diagonally across the field, making for the left-hand corner of the sports pavilion, or, if the pitches are being used, turn left to a wooden bridge and keep to the path on the right of the river. Cross the river by the next bridge and go towards the horse barrier by the roundabout. Re-enter Richmond Park for the car park.

For the longer walk (6¹/₂ miles)

At the corner of the fence with the windmill on the left, by a small white gate, cross the road and go through a green metal barrier and continue ahead. At a junction of paths, take the path slightly on the right marked 'No Cycling'. Keep on this path for about half a mile and then turn left on a path at the beginning of denser woodland leading down to the lake bordering the A3 called King's Mere. Turn left and keep along the shore towards the head of the Mere. Take the path leading through the trees, nearest to the busy road. Cross a drive to a house and go through some white posts and a gate very near the road. Just before the traffic lights ahead, cross under the road by the subway. A few yards past the exit to the subway, fork right on a grassy path which bends round to the right. Go left round the edge of a small pond and continue on a track. Fork left where the path ahead has street lights. You will soon see the tall spire of a church on the left. Keep left at an open space and then turn left towards the church, passing a group of pines by some cottages. Go down towards the road, passing a school on the left, and then the entrance to a church.

Cross Roehampton Lane and turn right towards the traffic lights, passing a water fountain and the Montague Arms (1745). At the traffic lights go left down Danebury Avenue and keep on this road to the riding stables at the end. The former village of Roehampton, once encircled by eighteenth-century mansions, is now swamped by the huge post-war housing estate, but Mount Clare (1772), with its fine position overlooking Richmond Park, can still be seen up on the left. At the riding stables, turn left to enter Richmond Park by the Roehampton Gate. Go straight ahead by the side of the road sign-posted to Sheen and Richmond and, after crossing the little bridge over Beverley Brook, turn left and skirt the edge of playing fields. Cross a stream in a ditch and go half-right on a path leading over another playing field at first and then on up towards White Lodge (home of the Royal Ballet School), which can be seen above the tree line. White Lodge was built in 1727-9 for George II and was the birthplace of Edward VIII in 1894. It has been used by the Royal Ballet School since 1955.

Keep on the path to the top of the hill, passing White Lodge on the right. At the far corner of White Lodge, Pen Ponds can be seen down on the right. Cross the grass towards Spankers Hill Wood, making for a path leading into the wood through a gap in the rhododendrons. Turn left at the first large clearing and then bear right on a path through the rhododendrons, emerging at a ridge overlooking the road to Pen Ponds car park. Turn left on the path circling the wood and go right on a path leading down by a small gorse plantation back to the car park at Robin Hood Gate.

11. Banstead Downs, Oaks Park and Woodmansterne

Distance: 6 miles.
Grid reference: 246604.
Ordnance Survey maps: 1:50,000 sheet 187; 1:25,000 sheets TQ 26/36 and TQ 25/35.

A fine breezy walk along Banstead Downs passing through two golf courses to Oaks Park and then on to Woodmansterne. The return to Banstead is made by field paths.
Bus: 164 (Morden to Epsom). Stop at Nork, near Banstead station.
Station: Banstead (SR). No service on Sundays.
Car park: Parking for a few cars at Banstead station, or park in minor roads at Nork. Turn off A2022 up Nork Way and immediately left up Eastgate, where there is parking on either side of the road.
Refreshments: In Nork, Woodmansterne and Banstead. There is also a cafeteria in Oaks Park open all year.

From Nork Way, cross the A2022 to take the cycle track opposite, which leads out to Banstead station. Cross the road and go down the footpath slightly right. Go over a crossing track almost immediately and follow the railway line up to the dual carriageway. Cross the road and ignore the footpath ahead. Turn left over the railway bridge and do not take the track immediately after the bridge, which is used by golfers, but take the next track which is a public bridleway leading through the golf course. Continue on the path, which narrows through a belt of trees, finally crossing over the railway line again by a bridge. At the junction of five or six paths on the other side of the bridge, take the second path from the left, going slightly uphill.

This path comes out to a road near a bus stop. Cross the road to take the footpath opposite, crossing a small road leading to a prison, after quarter of a mile. Take the bridlepath ahead and just before a residential road branch off to the right on a rather muddy path. Turn right along a small road and go through concrete posts at the end. There are fine views ahead here. Almost immediately turn left on a path leading past the gardens of houses with the golf course on the right. Keep on this path to a belt of trees which divides the course. Go through the trees and turn left on the main path leading down the wood. At the end of the path turn right on a track with a road on the left. Keep to the path nearest the golf course. Cross the road leading to the club house and continue on through the trees. On coming to a road going through Oaks Park, cross this and go diagonally right across the grass towards a

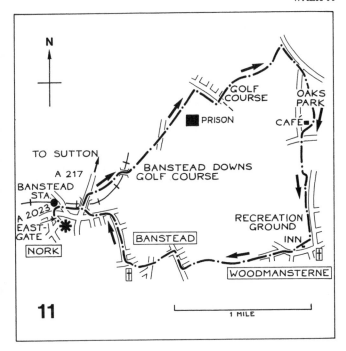

clump of trees. Continue on past groups of conifers and wall on the right to bend to the right to the cafeteria.

Leave Oaks Park by the white entrance gates and cross the Purley road to the stile opposite. Cross the field and go over two more stiles close together. Follow the path over the next field to a stile leading out to a road. Turn right down the road towards Woodmansterne. After a time there is a track on the right which avoids the pavement. This leads out to a recreation ground with the parish church of Woodmansterne ahead. Turn right on the grass past the tennis courts and continue up to the cricket pavilion. Take the path to the left of the pavilion out on to the road. There is an inn on the left. Turn right along the road to the second right-hand bend and go down Kingscroft Road on the left. At the end of this cul-de-sac, cross the stile and go over the top end of the field to the stile opposite to walk between wooden and wire fences. (Welsh ponies are bred on this farm.) Continue along this enclosed path and cross the stile at the end. Follow the path through the field, going diagonally right towards a kissing gate. Looking back there are fine views over Banstead Woods. Cross the next field in the same direction, following the grassy footpath past a low shed on the right out to a road.

Turn right along the road and after 300 yards turn left down a passage between Banstead Community Centre and Castle House. Go past the cricket ground to the gate and cross the road to take a small path opposite leading down to the churchyard and Banstead church. Take the path to the right of the church and branch right through the pampas grass out past the car park to the main road and shops. Cross the road and turn left to take the first turning on the right, Wilmot Way. At the end of this road, turn left at the main road and at the telephone kiosk cross the road to take a small footpath opposite. Keep to the left-hand fork. After 50 yards turn left on a narrow path. Turn left at the road which leads out to the main Brighton road by the railway bridge. Cross the road to take the path by the side of the line leading back to the station. For Nork, take the path on the left of the station, going past a small building. This leads back to the A2022, which you cross for the bus stop and car.

12. Along the Wandle from Morden to Wandle Park

Distance: 6¹/₄ miles
Grid reference: 259689.
Ordnance Survey maps: 1:50,000 sheet 176; 1:25,000 sheet TQ 26/36.

This walk follows the river Wandle from Morden Hall Deer Park, through Ravensbury Park and on past factories and mills which once made the Wandle 'the hardest worked river for its size in the world'. After passing through Beddington Park with its lovely herbaceous border and rose gardens, the walk ends at Wandle Park. There is much of interest to see along the route and there are no stiles or hills, and very little mud. The return journey is by train from Waddon Marsh to Morden Road. The trains run every half hour but please note that there is no service on Sundays.

Buses: 93 and 293. Stop by Morden Library on A24. Further buses at bus terminus in centre of Morden a short distance away.
Station: Morden Road Halt (SR, West Croydon to Wimbledon). Half-hourly, no service on Sunday. Cross the road and turn right to take a

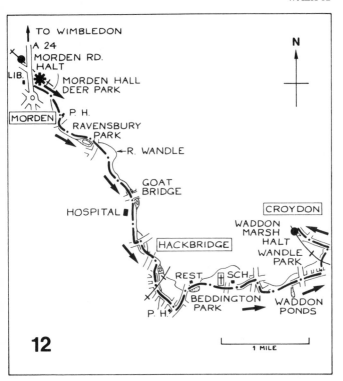

TO WIMBLEDON
A 24
MORDEN RD. HALT
LIB.
MORDEN HALL DEER PARK
MORDEN
P. H.
RAVENSBURY PARK
R. WANDLE
GOAT BRIDGE
HOSPITAL
HACKBRIDGE
CROYDON
WADDON MARSH HALT
WANDLE PARK
REST. SCH.
BEDDINGTON PARK
WADDON PONDS
P. H.
12
1 MILE

footpath signed 'Phipps Bridge'. After a few yards, turn right into the park and fork left after 200 yards (opposite petrol station), to join walk coming from library.
Car park: There is a slip road in front of Morden Library and Health Clinic on the A24, or, if this is full, parking is available in the side roads off the A24.
Refreshments: Various inns along the route. Restaurant in Beddington Park.

From outside Morden Library and Health Clinic on the A24, cross the road to enter Morden Hall Deer Park via a small wooden gate. The deer park is owned by the National Trust and is without deer at the present time. Take the path ahead with one of the channels of the Wandle (our first glimpse of the river) on the right. Cross the wooden bridge and then cross two more bridges straight ahead. Bear left over a bridge and continue down an avenue lined with trees, mostly limes and chestnuts. At the end of the avenue leave the park by the gate (public house on the left) and turn right for a short distance down the main road to a bend. Cross the road to take a path through railings to the left of the river. Cross by the second bridge and turn left into Ravensbury Park, soon coming to an attractive section of the Wandle with well kept flower beds and rustic fencing on either bank.

Do not cross the graceful bridge here but continue on to cross the first iron bridge over a channel. Turn right to follow the path past some attractive flats on the left, in front of which the stream has been widened to form a small lake. Go over another bridge and continue on to the London Road. Turn right for a short way, then cross the road to take a small path between hedges on the far side of the river, sign-posted Beddington Corner. The wooded area on the left is called Watermeads and is owned by the National Trust. It is carefully fenced off and is only accessible by key. It is partly used for willow cultivation. At the end of some playing fields on the right, the path forks. Keep to the left fork, shortly to reach the Wandle once more. One could imagine being in the heart of the countryside here and it is hard to believe that we are in the midst of a densely populated area. Turn right along the narrow, overgrown path, which soon widens. Large factories are evident now on the other bank but the path remains unspoilt. Snuff was once produced in the Morden mills in large quantities, about 6,000 pounds (2.700 kg) a month, and by 1805 there were five snuff mills using the river. On coming to a lane with a row of nineteenth-century millworkers' cottages on the right, continue out to the main road by Goat Bridge. Here there is an island full of historic mill sites. Paper, corn, logwood (for dyes), drugs and peppermint have all been milled here at various times over the centuries.

Turn right along the road and cross to a road marked 'Wandle Valley'. After a short distance, turn off left on a path by a stream, keeping to the left-hand section of the path for some way, then continue on a path past some blocks of flats to a road. Turn left over the road bridge and take the cul-de-sac on the right with a sign to Carshalton. At the end, turn down the footpath on the left, which leads to a small humpback bridge with an enormous factory away to the left. Cross the bridge and turn right to emerge on the main road. Turn right over the bridge and go left through an entrance in the railings to cross a green and take a tarmac path by the side of the river. This leads past back gardens and garages out to a small residential road. Turn left by the railings and follow the road out to Mill Lane. There is a brick bridge here leading to Wilderness Island, a Nature Reserve run by the London Wildlife Trust. Go under the railway and turn left over the road bridge. Follow the road round past a parade of shops and continue on this road down to the London Road, with an inn on the right. Turn left past a small public garden and after a short distance turn right by a public footpath sign into Beddington Park.

At the end of the car park go left into the park and turn left at the lake. Go over two stone bridges, bend round to the left over another stream and turn right. The Grange Restaurant is on the left. This serves lunches and has a fine outlook over the beautiful gardens. Go down the herbaceous border to the lake and turn left towards the graceful white bridge. Do not cross this but continue on to a stone bridge a little further on. Follow the path over the bridge and keep on this path through the park, going towards St Mary's church and the school, which was once a Tudor mansion belonging to the Carew family.

Cross the road leading to the school and continue on the path with a very old brick wall on the left. Go through some iron posts and out to Church Road. Follow this to the end and turn left towards the green and river.

Continue by the river down to Beddington Lane and at the bridge cross the road to take a footpath with the river on the left. Keep on this path, soon bending to the left and passing some small cottages with pretty gardens on either side of the river. At a T junction ahead, turn right to follow the road round to the left. At some stone posts at the end of the road continue ahead on a small metalled track. After some way the track emerges at an industrial estate with the beautiful Waddon Ponds Ornamental Grounds on the right. These ponds were once much larger and Nelson is reputed to have fished in them. This is our last glimpse of the Wandle.

Take the path past the ponds, up to the traffic lights ahead. Cross the busy Purley Way and continue up Waddon Road ahead. Just before a railway bridge, turn left down Vicarage Road towards a footbridge over the railway. Cross this and go diagonally left across Wandle Park to the entrance gates at the left-hand edge of the park. The Wandle was covered over here in the late 1960s and only the willow trees and a rushing sound from a manhole cover in the path give away its presence. At the end of the park, go through the gates and immediately take a path between wire fences on the left. Turn left at the end of the passage and go down a rather miserable road past rubbish tips to reach a residential road ahead. A short distance ahead can be seen the sign pointing down the passage towards Waddon Marsh halt. Trains run half-hourly (not Sundays) on a single track line from Wimbledon to Croydon West. Morden Road Halt is four stops along the line.

13. Kenley, Coulsdon Common and Happy Valley

Distance: 7³/₄ miles
Grid reference: 324601
Ordnance Survey maps: 1:50,000 sheet 187; 1:25,000 TQ 26/36 and TQ 25/35.

From Kenley station we climb steeply to the top of Riddlesdown and then walk across Kenley and Coulsdon commons to the beautiful Happy Valley, where several nature trails have been laid out by the City of London Corporation and the London Borough of Croydon. We return to Kenley via Old Coulsdon.

Bus: 197 (Norwood Junction to Caterham Valley). Stops on A22 by the turning to Kenley station.
Station: Kenley (SR; no service on Sundays).
Car park: Either at the station or in one of the side roads near the station. Turn right off A22 a mile south of Purley, by the sign to Kenley station.
Refreshments: Inns en route and in Old Coulsdon.

From Kenley station go up to the main road (A22) and take the footpath opposite with iron railings on the right, leading up a steep hill. After a few hundred yards, take the first clear turning on the left, going up through the trees. Go over two crossing tracks, soon emerging on the open downs called Riddlesdown. Turn right along one of the many grassy tracks, eventually to join the stony track leading down over the railway line to the main A22.

Cross the road to Old Barn Lane and go over the footbridge to pass a school with attractive recreation fields on the right. Cross a road and go to the end of a cul-de-sac to some steps. Near the top of the steps, turn right on a footpath. At the open common, with large signpost marked 'Kenley Common', cross a bridle track and go up to the ridge on a faint, grassy path. Continue in the same direction on a wide path between trees, ignoring a left fork almost immediately. At the end of the avenue of trees, continue on in the same direction, passing the end of a belt of trees, to the corner where the common and perimeter of Kenley Aerodrome meet. There is an active gliding club here. Go on to the unmade-up road and turn left on reaching a minor road. Almost immediately turn right down a small road or use the grassy parallel strip round to 'The Wattenden Arms'.

At the end of some houses on the left, turn left down a track with a

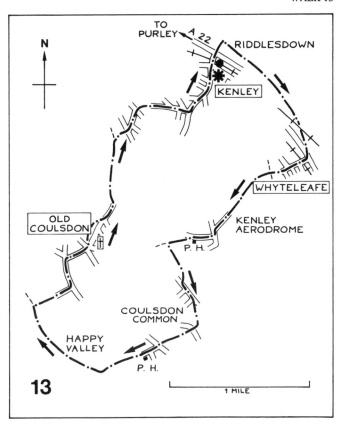

13

1 MILE

public footpath sign 'Access to the Haven'. When the metalled track swings away to the right, take the left fork slightly downhill, bending sharply to the left. Ignore a track on the right and continue ahead between posts on a narrow path past a cottage. Keep ahead some way through the wood, bearing left at a small T junction of paths. At a T junction with a house opposite, turn right downhill. At the road turn left up a 'no through road'. Just past a cul-de-sac, Rydons Wood Close, continue ahead and soon take a parallel path near the edge of the wood to the end of the road. In a few yards, turn right up a broad, grassy sward and, after passing a bench on the right, cross the small lane and immediately turn left across the road to take a path opposite leading through the trees. Ignore side turnings and, on coming to an open area, continue straight ahead past cottages on the left. At the road cross to the small road opposite and go diagonally right over the common to cut off the corner.

After the Fox public house and its car park, continue along the metalled road to a small car park on the left and a notice board on the right showing the layout of Happy Valley and Farthing Down. Croydon Council and the City of London have laid out various nature trails in this beautiful area and copies of the booklets can be obtained at the Fox during licensing hours and at the Welcome Tea Rooms near Farthing Down. Go down the metalled track past the notice board and almost immediately turn right to follow the path through the narrow belt of woodland parallel to the metalled track. At the end of this path cross over the track and go through a gap in the hedge. Go down the slope by the steps out into the valley bottom, turn right by the bridle track and then turn right again before the hedge which crosses the valley. Go into the wood and climb the steps to follow the path on to the down, cross path and steps to Post 9 ahead of you. Continue along the slope, with seats on the right, on to Post 10. Walk on through the gap in the trees into the next field and Post 11 on right, where there is a magnificent view of Happy Valley. Walk down the hill keeping to the hedge on the right to Post 12. Walk up the grassy slope towards Post 13. Wild flowers are abundant here, including some quite rare species. Follow the track up to Post 14 and here we leave the marked trail by turning left instead of right as the post indicates. Keep to the path by the side of the hedge on the right for some distance and take a right fork. At a crossing track in a wood, turn left down towards the valley. Just before reaching the bottom of the valley, turn right on a crossing track in the trees. On emerging into the open once more, across the valley you can see Farthing Down and the Welcome Tea Rooms, almost hidden by the trees. Continue in the same direction as before to a junction of tracks. Keep on the track by the hedge which swings round to the right under a wooden barrier. Go past Farthing Down Stables on the right and Toller Farm and shortly fork left out to a road.

Turn left and follow the road for about a quarter of a mile. At the main road, turn right, later seeing Old Coulsdon shopping centre and church. Cross the road bearing left to take the small road by the side of the war memorial, passing playing fields on the left and the church on the right. At the end of this pleasant residential road, turn left along a wooded path. Keep on this for some way, ignoring turnings, and in a broad dip continue over crossing tracks and take the left upper path at a fork. At the next small crossing track, with a beech tree on the left, turn right downhill into trees. Turn left at a T junction. At the road ahead, turn left and shortly right up Colescroft Hill. At the junction of roads, cross the road to some steps and continue in the same direction, through a thicket and bear right to an unmade-up road. Go along this stony lane to emerge at a road by a corner. Carry on ahead down the road to a main road. Cross this to Hayes Lane opposite. This leads past Abbots Lane to come out at a road by a corner. The bridge and railway station are ahead a short distance on the right.

14. Upper Warlingham, Farleigh and Selsdon Wood

Distance: 7¹/₂ miles
Grid reference: 342586
Ordnance Survey maps: 1:50,000 sheet 187; 1:25,000 sheets TQ 25/35 and TQ 26/36.

After a fairly steep climb to the top of the chalky slopes overlooking the recreation ground at Upper Warlingham, the walk continues along the downs to Farleigh, with an opportunity to visit the tenth-century church. Field paths lead to the beautiful Selsdon Wood Nature Reserve and the return to Warlingham is made through Kings Wood. Apart from the climb at the beginning of the walk, there are no more hills and very few stiles. Some of the bridle and woodland paths will be muddy and boots are advisable in wet weather.

Station: Upper Warlingham (SR). Hourly service on Sundays. Walk past the car park down the approach road to the B270 and turn right under the bridge. The recreation park where the walk starts is a short distance on the left.
Bus: 197 (Norwood Junction to Caterham Valley). Bus stop near traffic lights at Whyteleafe on A22. Turn left up B270 (if coming from Purley). The recreation ground is just past the railway bridge, on the left.
Car park: In the recreation ground at Upper Warlingham. At the traffic lights at Whyteleafe on the A22, turn left up the B270 (if coming from Purley). The park is a few hundred yards on the left, just after the railway bridge.
Refreshments: Inn at Farleigh and shops in outskirts of Sanderstead.

From the car park in the recreation ground at Upper Warlingham cross diagonally right towards a sports pavilion and tennis courts. At the courts continue straight on ahead and up the chalky slopes, keeping to a right fork on entering the trees. About halfway up there is a good viewpoint looking back over Warlingham. On reaching the top cross the field to the road and turn left towards a public footpath sign on the right by the side of Batts Farm. At the end of the footpath, by some cottages on the right, turn right through a gap leading to a large sports ground. Cross this to the middle of the hedge ahead and go over a stile to continue across the field to the left-hand corner and stile, turn left down the bridle track to the road. Turn left and take the first turning on the right (not counting the road immediately opposite the bridlepath exit). About halfway down this residential road, turn left on a narrow path by some conifers. At yet another park ahead continue forward on a tarmac path which swings round to the right, following a wire fence and a line of conifers. Go past the swings to the corner and continue on an enclosed path.

This path leads out to a narrow belt of woodland by a public footpath sign. Turn right along the bridlepath through the trees with the field on the right. Keep right at a fork. This track has been churned up by the horses from the nearby riding stables but after some way the soil changes to chalk and the track becomes much easier to follow. After crossing a beautiful shallow valley the track eventually emerges at the road at Great Farleigh green. The Harrow inn is a short distance on the right.

Cross to the green opposite and go diagonally left towards a footpath sign in the distance, just beyond a seat. A few yards past the sign there is a stile into a field, which you cross to another stile in the far corner. Turn right along the road for a few hundred yards. (If you wish to visit the tenth-century church of St Mary — usually kept locked, unfortunately — turn right at a footpath sign at the end of the some houses. Cross the field diagonally left to a stile and turn left to the church. Go down the lane to the road and turn left, past a farm, to a stile on the right. Do not take the footpath opposite.)

Just before a farm on the left turn left over a stile to cross a narrow field to a gate ahead. Follow the wide track between fences with fine views on the right towards New Addington. This track bends round to the left through a gate on to an enclosed waymarked footpath, and in about half a mile the path leads out to a road, but turn right immediately before the road down the bridle road to Courtwood Lane. At a wood keep to the left fork with a field on the left. This lovely path through the wood, with bracken and many spring flowers under the trees, eventually emerges at a road at the edge of a housing estate. Turn sharp left and go through tall green gates into the Selsdon Wood Nature Reserve.

This beautiful area is managed jointly by the London Borough of Croydon and the National Trust (the gates close at 4 p.m. in the win-

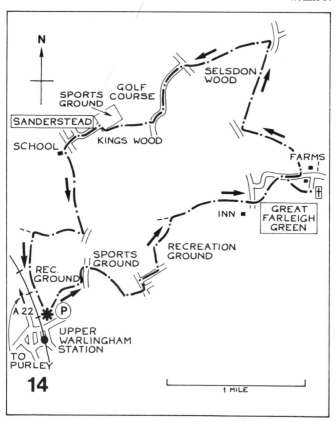

ter). Guides and maps of the Selsdon Wood reserve are available from the Chief Officer of Parks, Taberner House, Park Lane, Croydon, CR9 3JS (telephone: 081 686 4433). Take the path ahead going uphill and after a few yards fork left. Keep over crossing tracks and follow the path to open ground with a triangular wedge of woodland opposite. Keep left along the hedge and at the end of the woodland on the right cross an open area down to a gap in the trees, with views over Selsdon, and bear left on the path through another gap. Go across the grass on the path towards the car park, toilets and road.

Cross the road to Kingswood Way opposite and go up this private road, past the small flint cottage on the right named Cosy Corner, and on past many widely varying types of houses. Go through the white barriers across the road and continue ahead. When the lane bends sharply to the left, continue on for 20 yards, and then turn right through a barrier into Kings Wood. A Romano-British settlement, a small farmstead undisturbed for some two thousand years, was excavated near here in 1955 and 1959. A cemetery was also discovered, containing the remains of cremation urns.

Go forward on the wide track leading through the wood and turn first right. Follow this round to join a wood boundary, and down to a dip and the perimeter of a golf course on the right. Ignore a track on the left. Keep ahead on a path, soon with large sports fields on the right, to a T junction with a house on the right. Turn right up to some barriers out to a small road. Turn left and when the road divides keep left up to the main road, with a few shops on the outskirts of Sanderstead. Turn left and cross by the pedestrian crossing to take the small footpath leading up between houses and the school. The path bends round to the left past the back gardens of the houses and the playing fields of the school. At the end of the wire fence turn right for a few yards and then cross the field on the definite path. Go between the two fields through the gap in the boundary and continue on. At the end of the next field go through another gap and keep to the left-hand edge of the field to reach a road. Turn right down the bridle track.

After about half a mile, look out for a small boundary stone on the right. Turn sharply left opposite the stone (do not follow the diagonally right path across the field). After a few hundred yards, cross over a track and continue along with a thicket on the left. At a tree on the right turn off left on a path leading down the hill. You can now see the recreation ground and the station in the distance. There is a choice of paths down the slippery chalk slopes but they all lead out to the recreation ground and the car park. For the station turn right at the road and left immediately past the railway bridge. Keep on to the main road for the bus stops.

15. Lloyd Park, Addington Hills and Croham Hurst

Distance: 5¹/₂ miles (6¹/₂ from South Croydon station).
Grid reference: 338647.
Ordnance Survey maps: 1:50,000 sheet 177; 1:25,000 sheet TQ 26/36.

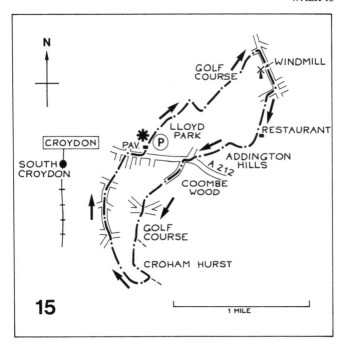

This attractive walk links some of the well known beauty spots near Croydon. From Lloyd Park we walk through the Shirley Park golf course to the Addington Hills, with a high vantage point overlooking south London. We then call in at Coombe Wood, 14 acres (5.7 hectares) of beautiful woodland and gardens with a nature trail leading past rock gardens, rose beds and herbaceous borders. A series of bridle tracks takes us to Croham Hurst, a wood containing a group of hut sites and a bronze age barrow and classed as a site of special scientific interest.

Station: South Croydon (SR). Leave the station on the west side, turn right on to a footpath alongside the car park. Fork left up to a footbridge and cross the line to continue forward along a series of passages, crossing four roads and another railway line, to arrive at the corner of Camden Road. Turn into the main Croham Road and go left

53

for a few yards to take a passage leading down to Lloyd Park in Coombe Lane. The car park in Lloyd Park is a short distance on the right.
Buses: Orpington and District from East Croydon station. Alight at Lloyd Park entrance. Green Line 853, 855, 857.
Car park: In Lloyd Park. Entrance in A212 (Coombe Road).
Refreshments: Addington Hills (cafe and restaurant — closed Mondays). Coombe Wood cafe. Also inns at Upper Shirley.

From the car park in Lloyd Park, go to the right of the changing rooms and cross the grass, passing the left-hand edge of a knot of trees in a depression, making for a line of trees ahead. At the narrow belt of trees, turn right on a path leading slightly uphill. Keep ahead on the path across the meadow, ignoring paths to the right, and at the end of the meadow go through a thicket. On coming out to the open again, keep straight on with trees down on the right. Do not go through the gap in the trees about half-way along but keep on forward. There are good views on the far left of the Crystal Palace television mast. About 100 yards before the wire fence to the golf course ahead, turn right at the end of the trees to follow the path downhill to iron posts and railings. Turn left along the track leading through Shirley Park golf course, keeping a watchful eye open for stray golf balls.

At the main road turn right for about a quarter of a mile, passing a windmill on the right standing in the school grounds. Continue past an inn at Upper Shirley to crossroads. Turn right by a telephone box and follow this road for 300 yards to a white house on the right. Cross the road to take a definite path in the woods by a telegraph pole. Bear right and keep on in a generally westerly direction for some way on a rising path gradually diverging away from the road. At a steep hill ahead take the stony, eroded path which leads to the brick viewpoint at the top of the Addington Hills, with magnificent views over south London and beyond. The various places of interest are marked on the semicircular wall and Windsor Castle can be seen on a clear day.

Follow the tarmac path to the restaurant and cafe. Just before the cafe turn right on a stony path. On entering a wood turn right to a shallow depression and take the rising path leading to a broad ridge path with steep slopes down into valleys on the left and right. Turn right on this path for some way to pass steep gullies down to the valleys. At the end of the spur take the left fork going downhill, keeping left to reach a crossing path at the bottom. Turn left along this path to a junction of tracks. Keep on in the same direction as before, going slightly uphill. Just before reaching the road, turn right on a main track running parallel to the road, passing a few trees marked with white paint. At the car park continue ahead to the main road and cross to Conduit Lane opposite.

Coombe Wood Gardens are on the left and these are well worth a visit. There is a cafe in the stable block where you can buy a leaflet giving the history of the gardens and details of a short ramble. A short resumé of the route is given here by kind permission of the Parks Department of the London Borough of Croydon.

After passing the pond on the left, bear left and you will come to the Rock Garden. Leave the Rock Garden through a gap in the Yew Hedge and you will enter the Rose Garden (donated by Nestlé of Croydon: some two thousand roses were to have been sent out to the public as part of a free offer, but a postal strike prevented this). Follow the curved path uphill into the Winter Garden. Immediately inside the Winter Garden take the path to the right that curves away under one of the large beech trees. Note the bed of fuchsia on your left with the pink-tinged foliage. Follow the low railing until you come to the top of the Broad Walk. Continue along this path, with the bed of hydrangeas on your right, and walk uphill until you come to a T junction. Turn right and then left and go up some steps to the top of the hill. Go down the long flight of steps on the opposite side of the hill. The hilltop is an outlier of the Blackheath Pebble Beds, as are the Addington Hills and Croham Hurst. Continue straight ahead and take the fourth path on your left, which will bring you back into the Winter Garden. Take the outer path past the cedar back into the Rose Garden and downhill under the archway in the Yew Hedge and you will see the mixed borders forming the Broad Walk. Continue downhill and you will come to the Terrace Garden. Bear right down the slope and you will discover an old farm wagon. Go under the brick archway to the stables, cafe and toilets. The horses belong to a team of mounted rangers who patrol sixteen of the large open spaces to the south of here. Retrace your steps to the main gateway and Conduit Lane.

Turn left down the lane, passing the Central Nursery (open to the public on Tuesday, Wednesday and Thursday afternoons) on the right. At the end turn right on a bridleway following the iron railings. At a white house by some footpath signs, continue forward downhill to Croham Valley Road. Cross the road with care and take the footpath opposite, marked to Croham Hurst. Just before the golf club house, go through the wooden barrier on the right to take the uphill track. On reaching the woods, turn left on a crossing track close to a parish marker. After 350 yards at a footpath notice high on a tree, turn right uphill through the trees to the top of Croham Hurst. There has been a wood here since the fourteenth century and because of this and its wide range of plant and animal life it has been declared a site of special scientific interest.

Turn right at the top along the stony path with fine views away to the left. At the open space there is a stone marking the site of barrows from the bronze age. A group of five hut sites are visible as faint enclosures on the east side of this open space. A variety of worked flints have been found here including an arrowhead and a scraper. Continue on in the same direction into the woods on a broad path (not the path by the escarpment). Soon the path drops down to reach a road, with another road called Bankside leading off on the right. Walk past Bankside to go down Croham Manor Road. At Croham Road turn left for South Croydon station (either following the road or retracing your steps along the series of passages). For the car park in Lloyd Park, cross the road to take the passage opposite, which leads down to Coombe Lane. The car park is on the right.

16. Keston Common, Leaves Green and Downe

Distance: 8, 6 or 5¹/₂ miles.
Grid reference: 419641.
Ordnance Survey maps: 1;50,000 sheet 177 or 187; 1:25,000 sheets TQ 46/56 and TQ 26/36.

From the beautiful lakes near Keston we cross the common to the windmill on the escarpment at Keston and descend the slope to take field paths and bridleways to the village of Leaves Green bordering the airfield at Biggin Hill. The walk can be shortened here to omit the village of Downe, for forty years the home of Charles Darwin, or a bus is available in Downe back to Keston if required (not on Sundays).

Bus: 410 (Bromley to Reigate). Bus stop on A233 by the edge of the lake at Keston.
Car park: On A233 about a mile south of the junction with A232 at Keston Mark. Large car park on the right at the end of the lake.
Refreshments: Inns at Leaves Green and Downe.

From the large car park by the lakes at Keston, take the path on the left-hand side of the lake at the corner of the car park, passing through a metal barrier and soon passing a seat After the causeway between the two lakes, turn left by the side of low wooden railings towards an open grassy area. Cross this in the same direction and take a path to the right

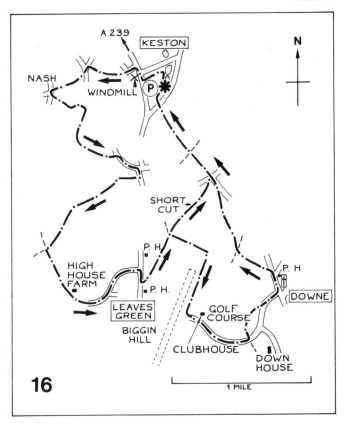

16

1 MILE

of the open area leading through the wooded common, with a minor road about 50 to 100 yards away on the right. At a crossing track go forward and at a small dewpond on the left fork left to take a small, grassy, rising path which emerges at the main road. Turn right past the war memorial and the windmill and cross the road to take the first road on the left (Leafy Grove). There are fine rural views here, especially in the winter. When the lane bends to the right, take the small path ahead between fences down by the side of the house.

This path leads down to a field. Bear right to an unusual metal stile and follow the grassy path between fences. Cross the field to another metal stile and follow the enclosed path to a road. Turn left down to a road junction, bear left and almost immediately take the footpath on the right. This path emerges at the small hamlet of Nash at North Pole Lane. Turn left and after a few yards take the footpath on the left by the side of a gate to Fortune Bank Farm, going over a stile. Cross another stile and keep forward down to the bottom of the valley. Follow the path round the edge of a field and keep on this pleasant path between fields for nearly a mile. After a while the path bends sharply to the left. On reaching the road turn right (if you look left at the view here, Crystal Palace mast is visible on a clear day). At Blackness Lane turn right and after 100 yards turn right again on a bridleway leading through a farmyard. Take the path on the right of a farm track.

After passing through apple orchards, the bridle track leads through fields and then into a belt of woodland. After a stile on the right, cross a stile on the left which has a footpath notice. Cross the large field diagonally right up towards High House Farm on the brow of the hill. The path is rather indistinct at first but soon becomes clear. This is a pretty valley. Go towards a gate and cross the stile to follow the path to the belt of trees at the top of the hill. Go up the farm lane (or turn right to a stile, do not cross this but turn left to cross a stile and follow the path to join the farm lane further on). The track leads on to a concrete drive past some farm buildings on the left. Follow the drive round to the left when it divides, passing some white houses on the right. After about half a mile we come to the common at Leaves Green, with a car park and some very superior toilets on the left. There are inns to the left and right on the main road.

Cross the main road and go over the green diagonally right towards some cottages and a stile by a footpath sign. Biggin Hill aerodrome is away to the right. Cross the field diagonally left out to a lane with a plethora of footpath signs.

For the shorter walk (5^1/$_2$ miles)

Go on the footpath across the large field ahead, under the pylons, and over a stile to an enclosed path leading out to a road. Turn right and at a road junction take the footpath on the left to join the longer walk at (A).

For the longer walk (8 miles)

At the footpath signs, go over the stile and take the enclosed path to Milking Lane, which encircles the outskirts of Biggin Hill aerodrome. At the first lane (Milking Lane) by a footpath sigh turn left, soon passing through the West Kent golf course, with the clubhouse on the left. This lovely course is set in another shallow valley. Follow the road across the valley and after climbing the steep hill look out for a footpath on the left, with another opposite. Follow the path on the left to a T junction and turn right. Cross two barriers and walk diagonally right over a field to go through a kissing gate and across another field. Go other a stile to an enclosed path leading out to a road.

This is the village of Downe, where Charles Darwin lived for forty years. His house, where he wrote *The Origin of Species* and made notable experiments with orchid cultivation, is a quarter of a mile away to the right and is open from 1 p.m. to 6 p. m. except on Mondays and Tuesdays; closed in February. Turn left towards the centre of Downe past the church, which has a sundial in memory of Charles Darwin. The bus stops here (not Sundays) and takes a few minutes to reach Keston (alight at the fork leading to Keston and walk up the main road, A233, or along the common to the car park by the lakes.) Catching the bus here cuts out 2 miles of the walk.

Turn left past an inn and several shops. Just past a road on the right, take the footpath signposted to Keston on the left, by a bus stop. Cross the field to a stile. Take the right-hand path leading away downhill through a beech wood. Cross the stile ahead down to a crossing track and bear right to a kissing gate to a field. Cross the field in the same line to a footpath sign opposite. Cross a stile and keep to the path with a wire fence on the left. On coming to the open field, keep to the left-hand edge and at the wood ahead turn right to go under the pylons. Cross a stile in the left-hand corner of the field to a road. Turn left to a junction and take the footpath opposite leading up the hill.

(A) Follow the path across the field, go over a private road and continue ahead on the path through a wood. This leads past a stone seat well placed for a view across the valley towards the hills opposite. There is a hollow tree trunk here with a young oak tree growing from the centre. After some way on this lovely path, cross the road to Keston Common opposite and follow the path in the dip on the right near the road. This leads back shortly to the car park.

17. Chislehurst, Petts Wood and Scadbury Park

Distance: 6¹/₂ miles or 5¹/₂ miles.
Grid reference: 432694.
Ordnance Survey maps: 1:50,000 sheet 177; 1:25,000 sheets TQ 46/56 and TQ 47/57.

This lovely walk, although quite close to urban areas, is almost entirely on footpaths through woods, commons and fields and there are some fine views but with very little climbing to be done. Chislehurst Caves are about a quarter of a mile from Chislehurst station and can be visited at the beginning or end of the walk if wished. Some of the woodland paths will be muddy after a wet spell. The shorter walk crosses the Scadbury Park Nature Reserve and visits a ruined, moated manor house.

Station: Chislehurst (SR).
Buses: 227 (Crystal Palace to Chislehurst). Green Line 725, 726, 755. Stop near Chislehurst station.
Car park: Free parking at Chislehurst station or in Gosshill Road (turning off A222 opposite the station approach road).
Refreshments: Some shops at Chislehurst West, towards the end of the walk and inn near Nature Reserve.

From Chislehurst station the caves are a short distance to the left, but we turn right towards the main A222 and cross by means of the pedestrian bridge. Descend the steps to the unmade-up lane, Gosshill Road, and turn left down this rough track passing a turning on the right leading under two railway bridges. At the end of a fence, turn left down a passage. Do not cross the bridge but turn right through a barrier on a small path following the stream. Follow this path for some way, with fields on the right, to a track leading over the stream up to Tong Farm on the brow of the hill. Turn right on the path leading between the fields and just before the railway line swing to the left, still following the path. At a footbridge over the railway, continue forward on the path. This soon enters Petts Wood, owned by the National Trust. Immediately fork left slightly uphill and keep right at another fork. Continue on this main path, ignoring side turnings. Go over a stream and at a sloping T junction turn right down towards the railway line. At the National Trust sign turn sharp left, slightly uphill, on the main path with the railway and foot tunnel on the right. Keep on the main path through the wood with a bridle track on the left. When the track almost joins the bridle way there is a National Trust stone which says that the woodland was saved in 1927 and given to the National Trust in 1957.

After passing a field on the left, continue forward at a junction of paths and cross a track. Cross over another track, to emerge eventually at a road. Go down the drive opposite and, just before some padlocked gates across the drive, take the track leading off on the right along an avenue of oaks and silver birches.

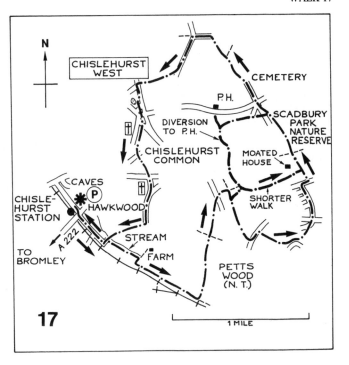

Alternative walk through Scadbury Park Nature Reserve

After 90 yards, turn left into the Reserve and at a T junction by Post 5 in 100 yards, one can either turn left to an inn for refreshments which is near an exit at Post 1 and return the same way, or turn right to keep on the main path ignoring signed exits. Go past a pond and turn left on a path signposted to the site of Scadbury Moated Manor. At the end of the moat follow the path back to the main path and turn left to rejoin the main walk at (A).

If you do not wish to go through the Nature Reserve follow the track past some playing fields on the left. Go up to a sloping cross junction, with a bench ahead, and turn left to a road. Turn left along this pleasant road for a short distance to a public footpath sign on the right just past some houses. Take the path across an open space with a seat and a fine view across to St Pauls Cray. The tarmac path soon swings round to the right, down a slope and up to a small road. Follow the road round the corner to a public footpath sign on the left. Go down towards the back gardens of some houses and, just before the fences, turn right for a few yards and then left down a passage which leads between the houses to a residential road. The following half mile is along quiet roads but we are soon out in the open country once more. Turn right down to a crossing road and cross to the road opposite, Breakspeare Drive, which leads to a main road at St Paul's Wood Hill. Turn right for a few yards and cross the road to take a footpath between houses.

(A) The shorter walk through the Scadbury Park Nature Reserve joins the main walk here by turning left along the enclosed path. At the top, at beautiful open country, if you wish to visit the Nature Centre turn right and follow the signs and return the same way (an extra half mile).

Cross the drive to follow the grassy path which leads clearly across the field, keeping quite close to the left-hand boundary. At the corner of the field, bend round to the left and follow the path up towards a cottage on the top of the hill. At the cottage keep to the fence. There are lovely rural views here. Go through a gate and down the drive to a busy main road. Cross with care to the small road opposite. At the end of this road take the path ahead, to the left of the cemetery.

When the path divides at the gates to the disused greyhound kennels, take the left-hand path. At the end of the kennels swing round to the left, go over a stile and cross the field to two stiles in the far corner. Take the left-hand stile and follow the enclosed path out through barriers to a slanting T junction. Turn left down to a lane and turn left again along the lane. On coming to some houses, take the footpath on the right between the first two houses. After passing some allotments this path leads out to a main road with shops. Turn left along the road for a few hundred yards and cross the road to a picturesque pond on the right with some seats and plenty of wildlife.

Take the path between the road and the pond and cross the small green to a mini-roundabout on Chislehurst Common, with the spire of a church visible ahead. Cross the roundabout diagonally to the green opposite and at another road cross this to take the path leading through the wooded common, with Prince Imperial Road and the church on the right. At a fork, after a few yards, take the left-hand path (not the bridle track). At another fork keep to the left-hand path. At a crossing path, about 75 yards before a road ahead, turn right. Turn left at a crossing track by a bench and follow the path between dried up ponds to a road. Cross the road to a path opposite with a wall on the right and soon emerge on to a private road. Bear left to the junction at School

Road. Turn right to cross the main road to go down Crown Lane, to a T junction by a Catholic church with a school opposite. Turn right past several schools and swing round a corner to the left. Ignore a footpath turning on the left and after 75 yards take a path on the right by the side of a drive. This lovely path, with panoramic views on the left, leads past a smallholding to Pond Wood. Take the path on the outside of the wood with a field on the right. This path goes gently down to the footbridge over the stream, encountered on the outward journey. Continue forward to the lane and turn right back to the station.

Index